TRANSFORMATIONS

Transformations
Your Inner Guide to Self-Exploration

iUniverse books may be ordered through booksellers or by contacting:

iUniverse
1663 Liberty Drive
Bloomington, IN 47403
www.iuniverse.com
1-800-Authors (1-800-288-4677)

ISBN: 978-1-4620-3316-4 (sc)
ISBN: 978-1-4620-3318-8 (e)
ISBN: 978-1-4620-3317-1 (hc)

Library of Congress Control Number: 2011911278

Printed in the United States of America

iUniverse rev. date: 8/4/2011

TRANSFORMATIONS

Your Inner Guide to Self-Exploration

MARK WILLIAM PEZZELATO

iUniverse, Inc.
Bloomington

To my parents, Gianna and Frank Pezzelato. Their wisdom, guidance, and support have given me the inspiration to create this beautiful work of art. They have shown me the true meaning of unconditional love.

You are the most important person in the world. After all, who do you spend the most time with?

Contents

INTRODUCTION

This work is written for all who seek joy, peace, and happiness. The goal is to provide a solid foundation for learning and growth. Through the six phases of transformation you will be prompted to contemplate, act, and be aware of your inner being. To put it simply, this book will change your life in unexplainable ways. We are entering a crucial time in the history of our planet, seeing the results of our neglect of nature. Our collective negative mind-set has plagued our existence for centuries. This book is designed to provide a source for spiritual growth and awakening. Use these words as a guide to inner development and true happiness. Your life can be lived only by you.

Read the following with an open mind and an open heart. The writings and teachings are meant to be contemplated. The topics are given on a day-by-day basis to allow time to absorb what has been said. It is best to read these passages in the morning and practice them throughout the day. Make it a habit to read one passage per day. Spiritual growth is the work of a lifetime. May your journey be that of happiness and prosperity. God bless you.

Phase I—Fundamentals

Basics, Habits, Thoughts, and Themes

Day 1
New Beginnings

"A journey of a thousand miles begins with a single step."

Lao Tzu

The start of a new year can be very inspirational and rejuvenating. This is a time of new beginnings. However, it is important to remember that new beginnings happen all the time. Every ending *is* a new beginning. You do not have to wait for a significant calendar date to change your ways.

Take time to reflect on a recent experience that has come to an end. Now notice the beginning that happened as a result of that end.

Day 2
Forgiveness

"There is no love without forgiveness, and there is no forgiveness without love."

Bryant H. McGill

Whatever happens, you will always be you. The loss of integrity and serenity is the price paid for not forgiving someone. Always practice forgiveness lest you lose your valuable energy.

Recall an instance when you felt unable to forgive someone. See if you still feel that way. If so, can you let it go? Can you forgive?

Day 3
Now

"I have realized that the past and future are real illusions, that they exist in the present, which is what there is and all there is."

Alan Watts

Now is the only moment you have. Living in the past, or waiting for the future, is the means to an end: the end to your happiness. Remember, all past and future events only happen in the *now*. Enjoy what you have, what you do, and whom you choose to spend your now moments with.

Throughout your day take notice when your mind trails off and stops paying attention to whatever is happening in front of you now. Quickly bring your attention back to the present moment.

Day 4
One

"We are one, after all, you and I. Together we suffer, together exist, and forever will re-create each other."

Pierre Teilhard de Chardin

We are the same entity, the same being. You are not superior, nor inferior. You are equal to every person regardless of occupation, status, or any other form of separation known in our society.

Next time you feel sorry for yourself or feel like nobody cares about you, remember that we are all one and the same, connected through divine essence.

Day 5
Empty Space

"All phenomena are empty."

Demosthenes

We are made of mostly nothing. If you were to take a single atom and enlarge it to the size of a stadium, the nucleus would be as big as a particle of dust in the center. Electrons the size of tinier dust particles would float around it within the vast empty space. It is through this nothing, this empty space, that all life exists. Look around. Something cannot exist without nothing, yourself included.

Take time to look around you. Notice how every room has empty space. Look outside and realize the vast emptiness that surrounds us constantly.

Day 6
Thoughts

"Thoughts are the shadows of our feelings—always darker, emptier and simpler."

Friedrich Nietzsche

You are divine essence, pure energy. The thoughts that flow into your mind are composed from your core beliefs and emotions. If you can observe your thoughts, you will come to the realization that you are not your thoughts. Your thoughts are the only things in life you can control.

The average person has about sixty thousand thoughts per day. Take notice when one appears in your mind. Can you let it go? The more empty space you create in your mind, the closer you are to eternal happiness.

Day 7
Goals

"Shoot for the moon. Even if you miss, you'll land among the stars."

Les Brown

There is something to be said for accomplishing a goal. No matter how significant the task, completing what you set out to do is a marvelous feat. It is far better to plan and achieve one goal than to plan and never finish several.

What sorts of tasks have you begun but have not finished? What are the next steps you need to take? What can you do right now to realize your dreams?

Day 8
Work

"All things are difficult before they are easy."

Thomas Fuller

We all need something to do with our time—something that gives us purpose and fulfillment. A job is work only if you see it as such. We work for many reasons, some of which are positive, others of which are negative. If you dislike your job and do it because you need the money, that is the wrong reason. If you do what you do because it makes you happy, and you would do it for free, then you are on the path to happiness.

Do you love your job? If not, what is it that you would really love to do? Why haven't you done it yet?

Day 9
You

"We begin to realize we are energy itself with all of its inherent possibilities."

Ted Andrews

What are you? Who are you? You are divine essence, pure energy. You are vibrations in their purest form, light. You are not more than nothing; you are less than everything.

Notice the infinite energy within yourself, how your body is a vessel that harnesses your true spirit. Feel the power within yourself.

Day 10
Stress

"Stress is nothing more than a socially acceptable form of mental illness."

Richard Carlson

Stress is a series of thoughts strung together over a long time. There is no space. No silence. This is the loudness of the mind taking over and running your life.

Do a forward bend. Think of nothing but your breathing. Long inhalation. Slow exhalation.

Day 11
Control

"If we are to go forward, we must go back and rediscover those precious values—that all reality hinges on moral foundations and that all reality has spiritual control."

Martin Luther King Jr.

Never do plans go according to plan. Never are expectations met. Never is the only time you will ever know.

Feel appreciation for the small aspects of your life.

Day 12
Friends

"So the last shall be first, and the first last."

Matthew 20:16

The people closest to you are a reflection of your true personality. If you love and admire the people who surround you, then you are a person of high regard.

Take notice of the people you spend the most time with. What are the qualities you love best about your friends?

Day 13
Scheduling

"A lot affects the outcome. It boils down to scheduling and the commitment of the network."

David Ogden Stiers

Making time for what is important to you is the fundamental difference between success and failure. If you put in the time, you will succeed. Whatever you make time for is what will grow and blossom. This is true for all aspects of life.

What are the important parts of life that make you whole? Are you making enough time during the week for them?

Day 14
Irritations

"The one who cannot restrain their anger will wish undone, what their temper and irritation prompted them to do."

Horace

We all experience feelings of unease or irritation. Whether you let it show or not, the feeling still arises. Where does this irritation come from? Why do you think this way? Is it really you who is agitated, or does it stem from somewhere else inside of you?

The next time you feel irritated, remember to look at yourself. Notice your thoughts and where they come from. It is not the person or situation that irritates you; it is the thoughts you equate with it.

Day 15
Unexpected Situations

"If one advances confidently in the direction of his dreams, and endeavors to live the life which he has imagined, he will meet with success unexpected in common hours."

Henry David Thoreau

Life is full of surprises. This is why life is so interesting and great. Sometimes situations arise that you never would have thought possible. The important point is that all situations happen in the now. Regardless of what *time* it is, you are in a particular situation. There is always something to learn from every circumstance.

The next time an unexpected situation arises, embrace it. Use the opportunity to take advantage of a new experience.

Day 16
Goals

"Our goals can only be reached through a vehicle of a plan, in which we must fervently believe, and upon which we must vigorously act. There is no other route to success."

Stephen A. Brennan

Did you set goals at the beginning of the year? Where are those intentions now? It's only been sixteen days. Goals are very important. You should have goals for every aspect of your life: vocation, health, money, family, leisure, things you want to do, and legacy. They will give your life purpose.

If you do not have goals, take some time today to write down exactly what you want. No dream is too big. If you have goals already, make sure you are reviewing them daily.

Day 17
Purpose

"I know in my heart that man is good. That what is right will always eventually triumph. And there's purpose and worth to each and every life."

Ronald Reagan

What does it mean to have purpose? What is your life's purpose? Why are we here? Who are we? To answer these questions, you must look deep inside yourself. What makes you happy? What do you love about life? How do you contribute to the outer world? Are you happy with your surroundings?

These are very important fundamental questions. This is the call to your first step on the journey to enlightenment.

DAY 18
FEAR

"There is nothing to fear but fear itself."

Franklin D. Roosevelt

We all experience fear in our lives—fear of performance, competition, rejection, pain, loss of a loved one, allergies, etc. The list goes on and on. Fear is an emotion. It stems from our beliefs. Fears are not who you are; they are a result of our limiting beliefs.

Is there something that gives you anxiety? Do you notice your heart beating faster as a result? Does your breath quicken? Does your body quiver? Take note of when these feelings arise. This is the beginning of your awareness of feelings.

Day 19
Freedom

"I know but one freedom and that is the freedom of the mind."

Antoine de Satin-Exupery

What does it mean to have freedom? In Western civilization we live in a society that tells us we are free because we do not give in to terrorism. However, this is only replacing doubt with fear. Freedom really means to be able to view your thoughts and emotions as a part of external life. Freedom is the awareness of the oneness within our true self.

Take a moment to feel your aliveness. Feel that you are not your body. You dwell within your body and radiate outward. You are energy in its purest form.

Day 20
Patience

"All human wisdom is summed up in two words—wait and hope."

Alexandre Dumas Pere

Being tolerant of someone or something is the minimum. To have patience takes practice and perseverance. Patience is to understand that situations are a result of the learning process. Patience is not external; it stems from within. Your thoughts are the cause of intolerance.

The next time you feel irritated or angered, realize that they are only emotions and have nothing to do with who you are. Remember, patience takes practice.

Day 21
Talents

"I have no particular talent. I am merely inquisitive."

Albert Einstein

We all have a passion for something in life. We all have a talent either explored or undeveloped that drives us. We all have a burning desire to be creative in some sort of calling. The trouble is, most people work jobs they don't like and never develop their talents. Most people become mediocre at hundreds of different talents as opposed to achieving major success in one aspect of their life that would make them truly happy.

What are your talents? What do you love to do? Are you making time for it on a regular basis?

Day 22
Karma

"How people treat you is their karma; how you react is yours."

Wayne Dyer

Karma is a universal law. It is not a feel-good principle. Everything you do has an impact on life, no matter what it is. Picture yourself in a bathtub filled with water. When you move your arms, the waves of the water push outward until they hit the sides of the tub. Then the waves come back to you in a greater degree as they accumulate and pass over the other existing waves.

If you make big mistakes, you will learn big lessons. If you make little mistakes, you will learn little lessons. Always put others first.

Day 23
Listening

"The first duty of love is to listen."

Paul Tillich

To listen to someone you must use your entire body. When people speak to you, feel their energy. Listen with your ears, watch with your eyes, and feel the sensations in your body change as they talk. This is real listening. You will find you will be of a lot more assistance to others in this way.

Being a good listener is the best help you can be for other people. Why do you think we were given two ears and only one mouth? Listen twice as much as you speak.

Day 24
Giving

"If you can't feed a hundred people, then just feed one."

Mother Teresa

Being a giver is truly amazing. When you can give something to someone without the need for anything in return, it is outstanding. Giving doesn't necessarily mean gifts. It greatly entails the little things. The biggest part of giving is putting others first in every situation.

Today when you go about your daily life, see the opportunities to give. Know that when you give, it is for the sole purpose of putting the other person first.

Day 25
Receiving

"Asking is the beginning of receiving. Make sure you don't go to the ocean with a teaspoon. At least take a bucket so the kids won't laugh at you."

Jim Rohn

There are two sides to everything in this world. With giving there is receiving. Unfortunate are those who are bad receivers. A lot of people take receiving for granted. Giving is just as important as receiving. To be able to appreciate what has been given to you is sometimes the hardest lesson to learn.

Every day, we are on the receiving end of something. The next time you are given a gift, recognize it and be grateful. You deserve it! That is why it was given to you.

Day 26
Eternal Life

"And who are you? Consciousness that has become conscious of itself."

Eckhart Tolle

Eternal life and internal life are one and the same. Who you are on the inside is the being that will forever live on. We are not human beings having a spiritual experience. We are spiritual beings having a human experience. Death is only an illusion, turning form into formless.

Death is the opposite of birth. Life has no opposite. Reflect on this.

Day 27
Law of Attraction

"All that we are is the result of what we have thought."

Buddha

Our thoughts become our reality. We manifest into our lives what we truly want and desire. Any known creation was a thought before it was a reality. You may think this is not true, because you do not have everything you want and desire. What stops you from having abundance are your limiting beliefs.

Do you believe your thoughts and what you talk about create your reality? Does your inner dialogue reflect your outer world? Take a better look.

Day 28
Intuition

"Intuition is the clear conception of the whole at once."

Johann Kaspar Lavater

There is a little voice inside ourselves. Some people call it gut instinct; others call it intuition. The more you follow your inner guidance, the more your inner voice will lead you. Your inner being knows what's best for you. If you have set goals and have been practicing the meditations of this journey, it's time that you listen to your inner self more. It will always lead you toward happiness.

As you go through your days, watch for moments when something inside you says to do things like, "Help this person." or "Share with this person." If the voice is telling you to cheat, lie, steal, or kill, that is the wrong voice!

Day 29
Bodies

"Take care of your body. It's the only place you have to live."

Jim Rohn

Our bodies are the vessels that allow us to live in this world. Most people neglect their bodies by feeding them poorly and rarely exercising. To be pure of mind, strong-willed, and present, regular exercise and a healthy diet are key. The better you are to your body, the better your life will become. You will be more confident, more energized, and above all, healthy.

There are many exercise programs that can help you achieve your goal, whether it be weight loss, strength, or endurance. It is very important that you be in great shape!

Day 30
Role Models

"People never improve unless they look to some standard or example higher and better than themselves."

Tyron Edwards

Having someone to look up to is very important. This goes for all aspects of your life. Choose your role models according to your goals. These people can be famous stars, or people you know. Interview them. If they are too famous to interview, then do research on them. Read biographies. Ask questions. How did they get to where they are? People love talking about their achievements. You can learn a lot from someone who has real-life experience.

Who are the people you look up to? Pick someone for each aspect of your life (career, spirituality, health, family, and legacy).

Day 31
Boredom

"Boredom: the desire for desires."

Leo Nikolaevich Tolstoy

Being bored is a state of mind. It means you are not yet fulfilled. Something is missing from your life. If you experience boredom, you are missing your life calling. How is this true? If you had found your calling, you would be satisfied with doing nothing. The days would never be long enough. Yet there would be no stress, because you would love every second of it.

The next time you feel bored, take a good look at your hobbies. What types of things do you love to do for fun? These do not include watching television!

Day 32
Habits

"Excellence is not a singular act, but a habit. You are what you repeatedly do."

Shaquille O'Neal

We are creatures of habit. We all have routines and daily rituals that we follow. For instance, it is a good idea to brush and floss your teeth every day. It is not good to consume a lot of alcohol every day. It is said that you acquire a habit after repeating it for at least thirty days in a row.

Do you have something you would like to start doing on a daily basis that would contribute to your well-being? Jogging perhaps? Start now.

Day 33
Quiet Time

"An inability to stay quiet is one of the conspicuous failings of mankind."

Walter Bagehot

It can be difficult to find time for yourself. With our fast-paced lives, we sometimes forget about the little things. Most of us wake up and frantically rush around to get ready for work. At work, the day never seems to end. By the time we get home, we are exhausted, only to find a new set of responsibilities. As soon as there is a free moment, it's to the television we go.

It is very important that you find at least ten minutes of quiet time for yourself per day, with no interruptions. This is the bare minimum to keep your sanity. It can be at any point in the day or night. Use this time to calm yourself, breathe, stretch, and meditate. Zero distractions.

Day 34
Opposites

"Our mind is capable of passing beyond the dividing line we have drawn for it. Beyond the pairs of opposites of which the world consists, other, new insights begin."

Hermann Hesse

We live in a world of opposites. Good and bad, happy and sad, darkness and light, love and pain, birth and death. Yet we sometimes forget this phenomenon. We always want things to advance forward. But this will never happen. We will always experience loss, emotions, and shortcomings. This is life, and it's all in the way you view your reality.

The next time a situation occurs that you find unpleasant, remember, it is neither good nor bad. It just simply is.

Day 35
Viewpoint

"A purely objective viewpoint does not exist in the cosmos or in politics."

Howard Fineman

Your point of view is the equivalent of being at the bottom of a well looking upward at the sky. You are able to see only a little portion of the sky and know of nothing else. As individual human beings we know little. We have tunnel vision. If we could only see past ourselves and mind our surroundings, maybe then our view would broaden. We need to see the world outside of the well. However, the more you consider only yourself, the deeper you sink.

Notice the beauty around you. Flowers are a good start. Relax and enjoy the precious moments you have and share.

Day 36
Cleanliness

"A person might be an expert in any field of knowledge or a master of many material skills and accomplishments. But without inner cleanliness his brain is a desert waste."

Sri Sathya Sai Baba

Picture your living space surroundings as your mind. Every day your brain accesses millions of bits of information. If your mind was cluttered with ongoing needless thoughts, it would not be able to process information as efficiently. You can know a lot about someone and their mind-set by how clean their surroundings are. If their bedrooms or workspaces are piled with clothes or papers, and there is no space anywhere, chances are they are very frantic and stressed. If there is no space around you, how can there be space in your mind?

Take a good look around. Is everything in its right place? Have you made order out of your daily chaos?

Day 37
Judgment

"Everything that irritates us about others can lead us to an understanding of ourselves."

Carl Gustav Jung

One of the most difficult lessons to learn is regarding the judgment of others. We go through our days and see people make mistakes, or say things we don't like, or act in ways we fail to understand. Know that we are all individual and unique and we're all trying to attain the same goal: eternal happiness. When you judge someone, you are actually finding a character flaw within yourself. To judge or ridicule gives life to your ego. What's more, your ego will never be eternally happy. It is impossible because your ego lives only in this external world of opposites.

The next time your mind or mouth judges someone, stop. Take a deep breath. Realize that what you do not like about that person is not something to do with that person at all. It is something within yourself that is the issue.

Day 38
Focus

"Your focus determines your reality."

George Lucas

What writes better, ten dull pencils or one sharp pencil? The sharp pencil of course. The same analogy can apply to your life. Is it better to be mediocre at ten things, or to be excellent and successful at one? Successful people have something in common: focus. They realize the value of being extremely good at what they love. It is sometimes hard to focus on one aspect of life because there are so many things we could be doing.

The reason why you are excellent at your job is because you spend at least forty hours a week doing it. The same goes for any hobbies you love. Become really excellent at one thing, and you will be acknowledged and admired.

Day 39
Music

"After silence, that which comes nearest to expressing the inexpressible is music."

Aldous Huxley

Our bodies were designed to hear and feel music. It is so vital to our well-being. It is amazing how so many people take for granted such a wonderful creation. Music is a universal language that speaks to us on so many different levels. It is music that encourages people to dress in certain styles, act in different ways, and feel various emotions. Songs are our voice when we cannot find the words to express ourselves. Music is vibrations that make us move and come alive.

Always welcome music into your life and enjoy yourself. Move around. Have some fun! Your soul will thank you.

Day 40
Love

"The most important thing in life is to learn how to give out love, and to let it come in."

Morrie Schwartz

Love is deep down within you. It is compassion, patience, and tolerance. Love is our strength in times of adversity. Love is not an emotion; it is a state of being. Love for one another and our planet is our only chance for survival. We are responsible for our actions. We are responsible for the lack of consideration of our fellow beings. It all starts with ourselves.

Look at yourself. You are beautiful. You are one with all beings. You are important to our survival.

Day 41
Anger

"A man is about as big as the things that make him angry"

Winston Churchill

A lot of people get angry on a daily basis. Some people are to the point where they are unapproachable. Do you think that person is truly happy? Anger happens because we think we have a right to be agitated. We have a right to treat others poorly. We have a right to lose our temper. Regardless of the situation, there is never a reason to be angry. Anger is only a reaction that feeds the ego.

Before an angry reaction, your body will experience an unpleasant feeling. The anger is simply a reaction to this feeling. Notice sensations in the body and take responsibility for your reactions to them.

Day 42
Disappointments

"The size of your success is measured by the strength of your desire; the size of your dream; and how you handle disappointment along the way."

Robert Kiyosaki

Life is filled with disappointments. Actually, you will always be disappointed if you have expectations. We all think situations will go a certain way, but they rarely do. We expect certain outcomes and rewards for our hard work and time. Life is not so black and white. This is why people get so caught up in the monotony of everyday life. They never take risks, because they are afraid of the outcome.

Let go of expectations, and the results will follow. A disappointment is a non-existing way of living. There is no such thing as a good or bad outcome. Everything simply is.

Day 43
Meaning

"If I asked for a cup of coffee, someone would search for the double meaning."

Mae West

We are all in search for deeper meaning, the way of life. Value occurs only when we give something meaning. For instance, when the clock reads 11:11 we make a wish, or think, *That's odd; it's 11:11.* Realistically, the only value the clock time has is to you. You gave it meaning because you thought it was significant. Just like your horoscope. If something you read strikes you as important, then it must be significant, right?

Life is filled with coincidences. They can be positive or negative, depending on your point of view. Is the glass half-empty or half-full? Is your life significant or not? The point is that every moment of every day is a meaningful event.

Day 44
Food

"Are you eating it? Or is it eating you?"

Larry Cohen

We all know that what we eat is important. However, in Western society there are many people who are overweight. Eating properly is a starting point. It is the beginning of experiencing true happiness. If you eat what is good for your body, it means you care for your body and what has been given to you. It shows appreciation and love for you.

Do you eat healthy foods? Do you look at the ingredients and percentage amounts on the side of the box before buying products? Do you care about your well-being? The world needs you to care!

DAY 45
FAMILY

"Other things may change us, but we start and end with family."

Anthony Brandt

It is said that you choose your friends, but you were given your family. The idea of family is amazing. It is an unconditional love between humans. Family is the most important bond you have. Friends and relationships will always come and go, but family is forever. They are with you wherever you go and care for you deeply. However, not everybody is so lucky to have a loving family. Those are the people who need the most love.

Appreciate your family—the bond you have with each person. It is so vital to our existence because it is the very basis of unconditional love. If a family is what you lack, you are very special indeed. You are free to help others in selfless ways with no attachment.

Day 46
Ideas

"An idea that is developed and put into action is more important than an idea that exists only as an idea."

Buddha

Do you have a way of recording your ideas? Ideas are the starting block of independence and fortune. Ideas come to us from the divine. Everything in this world was first an idea, and then was acted upon to become reality. Make sure you always have pens and paper with you at all times. It is also good to have a personal recording device for inspirational moments.

Ideas are the seeds of the future. No idea is bad. Write it all down. Always keep paper and a pen with you to capitalize on your creative nature.

Day 47
Goal Check #1

"Vision without action is a daydream. Action without vision is a nightmare."

Japanese Proverb

Have you been reviewing your goals? Did you even set any goals? What are you doing to accomplish them? This is very important to your well-being. Most people have no aim or purpose. They keep going around in circles working jobs they don't like, only to make barely enough money to survive.

Plan your future. Write out your dreams as if they have already come to fruition. Find pictures that accurately portray the goals you are attempting to attain. Review your goals daily.

Day 48
Past

"Stop acting as if life is a rehearsal. Live this day as if it were your last. The past is over and gone. The future is not guaranteed."

Wayne Dyer

Sometimes it is hard to let go of the past. There are some instances when we may have been abused. There are other situations that were so good we try to relive them over and over again. We live in the past when we bring it to life through thoughts and words. However, the past has no place in the present. Yes, your past carves your experiences, but it has no relevance to your life right now. Even as you read this the moment has gone.

All you have is now. All you are is now. To relive the past is playing role to ego. Clear your thoughts and be right here, right now.

Day 49
Laughter

"Why so serious?"

The Joker in Batman

Surely you've heard that laughter is the best medicine. This is very true. When was the last time you laughed so hard you cried? When was the last time you were rolling on the floor in laughter, holding your belly? Do you laugh at least once a day? If you have to schedule in your laugh time, you are doing something wrong. There is always something to laugh about. Smiling, laughter, happiness, goodwill, positivity; they are all very important to our well-being. Life is worth living.

Recall a moment of joy and happiness. Sit with it for a few minutes and experience all the pleasant sensations associated with that moment.

Day 50
Religion

"Religion is to do right. It is to love, it is to serve, it is to think, it is to be humble."

Ralph Waldo Emerson

One thing that all religions have in common is the message of love. That being said, religion is important to our way of life. You do not have to believe in a specific religion to be kind and compassionate. However, some people need religion to help with their lives. Over the years, religion has got a bad reputation. It seems that people have missed the point. It is neither right nor wrong to go to church and believe in God. It is our natural way of life that is the issue.

Religion helps make us believe in what we cannot see. All people are entitled to their own ways of life, as long as their intentions are good. Do you believe in God?

Day 51
Experience

"Experience is the name everyone gives to their mistakes."

Oscar Wilde

Nothing beats experience, no matter what the calling. In everything we do, the person who succeeds is the one who has experience. Too often we try something new for the first time. We then expect results right away. We expect to learn new skills quickly and easily. This is a misconception. We see success in others and wonder why it is not ourselves who is in the spotlight. Your time will come when you have the experience and know-how.

You deserve everything that comes to you and everything that does not. What kinds of experiences would you love to have?

Day 52
It

"Forever always seems to be around when things begin, but forever never seems to be around when they end."

Ben Harper

There is something far greater than us. You can feel it. You can see it. You can be a part of it. We are superior as a whole. Together forever.

Can you feel your aliveness? Your body is changing moment by moment. Sit in silent stillness and experience your ever-changing reality.

Day 53
Help

"Never do something yourself that someone else can do better."

Henry Ford

For some people asking for help is hard to do. It all starts with the little things, like asking for help when you need to lift something heavy. Or asking for assistance on a project you are doing. In any case, to be successful you need the help of other people. In fact, whatever venture you pursue requires other people to survive. Other people's help is what keeps us interconnected. Without other people, life would be meaningless.

Do you have trouble asking for help? Remember you cannot do everything yourself. All successful people use the help of others to achieve greatness.

Day 54
Control vs. Command

"To get up each morning with the resolve to be happy … is to set our own conditions to the events of each day. To do this is to condition circumstances instead of being conditioned by them."

Ralph Waldo Trine

It is impossible to control. However, we can command. Orders can be met, and we can lead. Have you ever noticed that as soon as you try to control something, you lose control? On the other hand, if you relax and let whatever it is happen, it naturally falls into place. Command is something we as humans were born to do. We can command great ideas into existence. All we need is belief in ourselves.

Do you try to control people or outcomes? Do you get upset when things don't go your way? Just relax. Take a deep breath. Everything simply is.

Day 55
Learning

"God allows us to experience the low points of life in order to teach us lessons we could not learn in any other way."

Stanley Lindquist

It is said that every day we learn something new. Did you know that you can learn something from everyone? Every person you come into contact with has something to teach you, whether you believe it or not. How can this be true? Everyone has different experiences and therefore always has something new to share with the world. Even children can teach you great lessons. In fact, children are great role models for learning to live in the present moment.

The next time you cannot find the deeper meaning of an encounter, stop. Try to find the lesson to be learned. Always ask yourself; What can I learn from this person?

Day 56
Humbleness

"The praise that comes from love does not make us vain, but more humble."

James Matthew Barrie

What does it mean to be humble? In our society humbleness is misinterpreted. Some people think being humble means to not deserve rewards or kind words of praise. This is not the case. To be humble is to realize your true talents and potential—to know you are one with everything and therefore your talents are an extension of divine creation. When you accept rewards and words of praise with an open heart for a job well done, that is humbleness.

How are you humble? Do you realize your talents as a gift? Do you help others, searching for nothing in return?

Day 57
Trees

"That's one small step for a man, one giant leap for mankind."

Neil Armstrong

Picture a tiny seedling in the palm of your hand. You walk over to a patch of dirt and plant the seed. Eventually, the seed takes root and sprouts through the soil. Years pass and what could once fit in the palm of your hand is now a beautiful, healthy tree. If you were to watch a tree grow, it would be a very slow process. The tree takes its time, becomes strong, and creates a sturdy foundation. It makes progress in small stages not visible to the human eye.

A tree grows like your experiences. To be a talented, successful individual, you must take little steps. What are your next little steps?

Day 58
Equality

"All men are by nature equal, made all of the same earth by one Workman."

Plato

We are all equal, but in today's society this concept seems difficult for most. What does it really mean to be equal? We segregate ourselves through class status, marital status, gender, race, money, etc. For some reason we attach ourselves to our outer reality and think we are above it all, that the mistakes of the world are made solely by others. To be equal is to treat others like royalty, to put others first.

Wherever you go and whatever you do, put others before yourself. At first it may seem difficult. Eventually, you will be anxious for the next opportunity to shine.

Day 59
Consciousness

"The modalities of awakened doing are acceptance, enjoyment, and enthusiasm."

Eckhart Tolle

It is said that true happiness comes from being conscious. What does it mean to be conscious? It means to be present, to not get lost in thought. We have thoughts, but they are not who we are. Consciousness is like a flowing stream with no beginning and no end. We are like a drop of water in the stream of consciousness. We are consciousness aware of itself and, therefore, the product of awakening.

Take a moment to be aware of your surroundings. Pause in stillness and experience this moment without labeling or personalizing.

Day 60
Extra Days

"They've got an extra day."

Debbie Johnson

February 29 is an extra day that comes but once every four years. There is no such thing as days, weeks, months, or years. All we have is now. This seemingly extra day is put in place to somehow provide balance and order to the seasons. If you really stop to think about it, each day is no more than a repeat of the last. The only difference is what you do with the day you are given.

Enjoy your extra day. Enjoy every day. We are all fortunate to be here for at least one more day.

Day 61
Water

"Water is life's mater and matrix, mother and medium. There is no life without water."

Albert Szent-Gyorgyi

Water is very interesting. It can be a liquid, solid, or vapor. We are made up of approximately 70 percent water. On a daily basis we change how we look and feel. Situations change as the days go by. However, life always moves on. Things come and go. Water flows. No matter how many transformations water encounters, it can always come back to being water. Water gives life. Water is essential to our life on earth. It changes as the days go by. Just like us. We are part water, and water is part us.

Take the opportunity to observe the natural flow of water from a stream, lake, or river. Feel its vibration. Calm your mind.

Day 62
Form and Formless

"The pure impulse of dynamic creation is formless; and being formless, the creation it gives rise to can assume any and every form."

Kabbalah

If you were to look around, you would see we are surrounded by two types of matter: form and formless. Form is anything with pattern or geometrical shapes; for instance, circles, squares, usually man-made objects. Then there is formless. Some examples are snowflakes, blades of grass, and trees. Our world combines form and formless. Every object contains both. For example, if you were to look at an individual floor tile closely, you would notice that it is different from all the others. Its makeup is different and unique. However, if you were to stand back and look at all the floor tiles at once, there would be form and unity.

Look around and notice the form within the formless, the chaos amongst the stillness. This is life. Even in ourselves, the human body, there is form and formless.

Day 63
Late

"Better three hours too soon than a minute too late."

William Shakespeare

"You'd better hurry up, or you're going to be late." "What time is it?" "I'm not going to make it to work on time." Where does all this come from? Yes, we do live in a time-based reality. This is a world where we use minutes and seconds to give order to our lives. Being late for something makes us act differently. It is common that if someone is late for something, he or she may tend to rush or worry. Have you ever noticed that when you arrive somewhere, life still went on regardless of whether you were on time or not? It is always good practice to be on time, but it is not the end of the world if you are running late.

The next time you're going to be late, relax. Take a deep breath. Make a phone call to the person you need to meet if you have to. Just don't make being late a habit.

DAY 64
PERMANENCE

"Strong character is brought out by change, weak ones by permanence."

Jean Paul Richter

There is no such thing as permanence in this reality. Everything comes and goes: friends, family, material possessions, talents, etc. The only aspect of life that is permanent is your divine energy, your soul. We live on forever with no beginning and no end. It is form that we attach ourselves to. We are life, and it is worth living.

Enjoy what your life has to offer now, because it is anything but permanent. Be thankful for the little things.

Day 65
Depression

"Depression is nourished by a lifetime of ungrieved and unforgiven hurts."

Penelope Sweet

Many of us go through something called depression. This is when we train ourselves to think of only the negative. Most people experience depression on a small scale. They get depressed from time to time, depending on their moods or what they are thinking about. This may shock you, but there is no such thing as being depressed. It all has to do with your state of mind. Some people are diagnosed as depressed because they have been thinking negatively for so long that they fail to break the habit.

Depression is a sickness of the mind. Negative thoughts lead to depression. Try to catch yourself the next time you think negatively. Replace the thought with something positive.

Day 66
Purchases

"Many a man thinks he is buying pleasure, when he is really selling himself to it."

Benjamin Franklin

Interestingly, you will find as you become happier with your life, you will make fewer purchases. Sure, you will always have to pay the bills, buy food, keep up with maintenance, and so on. But the wants and desires will disappear. It is really, truly amazing. The happier you are, the easier it is to save money, because you will no longer have needless wants. Your purchases become smart choices that reflect your inner wealth.

Enjoy what you have, be it material possessions or family and friends. You will find that you will be less selfish and the purchases you make for yourself will diminish over time. You already have everything you need right now.

Day 67
Dreams

"You see things, and you say, 'Why?' But I dream things that never were, and I say, 'Why not?"

George Bernard Shaw

When we go to sleep at night, we enter a state of unconsciousness. During the time we are at rest, we go through many different phases of brain activity. The deepest dreaming phase is known as REM sleep, or rapid eye movement sleep. This is the time when we experience our subconscious mind talking to us through images and events. These symbols serve as a guide because they are given to us from higher consciousness. Even though we sometimes cannot fully understand the meanings of these dreams, they are rich with information pertaining to our lives.

When you dream in the middle of the night, make sure you have a pen and paper ready to write down your results. Make some point form notes, and then go back to sleep. Dreams are your subconscious mind's way of communicating with you.

Day 68
Balance

"Life is like riding a bicycle. To keep your balance you must keep moving."

Albert Einstein

There are two types of balance, and they are both interconnected. The first is actually physically balancing. This is often practiced in Yoga and is very helpful for clearing the mind. Balancing strengthens your core muscles and focus. The second form of balance is in your life. Make time for what is important to you. Ensure the right amount of work and play during the day. Make time for family and friends. Enjoy life as it unfolds.

Are you balanced? Do you make time for family and fun? Life is meant to be enjoyed.

Day 69
Thank You

"Just a 'thank you' is a mighty powerful prayer. Says it all."

Rosie Cash

The two words *thank you* are very powerful. They convey the message that you are grateful for what you have attained. Look around; you have plenty to be thankful for. The first step to attracting what you want in life is to be appreciative of what you already have. Your mind is filled with clutter. It says things to you on a daily basis you could do without. Replace your negative thoughts with the words *thank you.* Soon you will notice a profound difference in the way you feel and in your external reality.

Make an effort to continually repeat in your mind the words thank you. Try this in the morning and before you go to bed at night.

Day 70
Pleasure

"The noblest pleasure is the joy of understanding."

Leonardo da Vinci

Everyone wants to live a life of pleasure. However, for most it seems virtually impossible. There is always an excuse. What is life all about? We are here to be happy. Keep in mind that pleasure does not mean using people, taking drugs and alcohol, or partying all the time. To experience pleasure, one must be happy with his or her surroundings and take the time to relax and enjoy the moment now as it unfolds.

Feel the moment now as it is. Feel the pleasure of life. Realize that you are a miracle and you deserve the very best from yourself and the world.

Day 71
Birthdays

"It takes a long time to grow young."

Pablo Picasso

A birthday is a time for celebration. It's a time to feel special and be thankful for the gift of life. Some people get depressed when another year rolls around. How can you be depressed about celebrating life? Birthdays are a great way of getting together with family and friends and enjoying the fact that you're alive. If no one is planning your birthday for you, why don't you plan something for yourself? It's your day, and you can do what you want with it.

You do not need an excuse to feel special and appreciated. You should be thankful for your life every day.

Day 72
The Extra Mile

"No one ever attains very eminent success by simply doing what is required of him; it is the amount and excellence of what is over and above the required that determines the greatness of ultimate distinction."

Charles Francis Adams

Whenever you do something, do it with your full attention. Go the extra mile. Do more than the bare minimum, and you will begin to notice something truly amazing. People will acknowledge the great work you are doing and reward you accordingly. You will be compensated more for your efforts. You will build greater trust in relationships. Plus, people will help you in whatever you need for no charge, because they know you would do the same for them. No one ever complains when you do extra for them.

The next time you have to give your time or services, look for ways of going the extra mile. See if you can give more to that person for the pure selfless act of giving.

Day 73
Athletes

"We all have dreams. But in order to make dreams come into reality, it takes an awful lot of determination, dedication, self-discipline, and effort."

Jesse Owens

Incredible are the talents of humans. When one focuses on a specific goal and works towards it with tireless effort, one becomes an athlete. Athletes are the bright stars in the sky. In the midst of darkness, a star is born. An athlete is not just in the Olympics. There are gifted people in every form of life. There are people who stand out in their work environment. People who are gifted at music, visual arts, photography, sculpting, or entrepreneurship are amongst the greatest of athletes.

What is your focused talent? Do you strive to become an athlete?

Day 74
Child

"How sharper than a serpent's tooth it is to have a thankless child."

William Shakespeare

As children we eventually become accustomed to our parents. We start to feel we know better and end up telling them how something is done. We forget that they raised us, gave us life, and are wiser in their years. Some people will say, "Well, my parents do not deserve respect; they were not good parents." Ask yourself, "How can I be a good child to my parent now?" Forgiveness is one of our greatest life lessons.

Embrace your mother and father with open love in your thoughts. Forgive if necessary. Forgive yourself. Love and be loved.

Day 75
No

"No one saves us but ourselves. No one can and no one may. We ourselves must walk the path."

Buddha

How many times have you heard the word *no*? Too many to count, right? No seems to appear more often in people's vocabulary when you are asking for something out of the ordinary. When you want to succeed at anything, you will often hear the word no. The trick is to keep asking until you get a yes! Eventually you will get a yes; it is inevitable. It's like bowling. If you throw the ball down the lane enough times, no matter what caliber bowler you are, eventually you will get a strike.

Someone saying no is most often the worst scenario that could happen. You will just be in the same position as when you started, so you might as well ask.

Day 76
Promises

"The best way to keep one's word is not to give it."

Napoleon Bonaparte

When you make a promise to somebody, it is very important that you keep it for two reasons. The first reason is for the other person. If you promise to be somewhere and don't show up, you are proving to be unreliable and they will not take you so seriously the next time around. The second, and most important reason, is for yourself. When you make a promise and break it, your words hold less meaning. This also affects your day-to-day life and what you manifest into reality. If you continually break promises and are false to your word, when you ask for something from the divine, chances are you will not get it. Why? Because deep down inside not even you believe what you say.

Always keep your promises. If you cannot fulfill your word, make good by apology, honesty, and integrity. Never promise what you cannot deliver.

Day 77
Drinking

"Cigarettes and coffee: an alcoholic's best friend!"

Gerard Way

There will always be an excuse to drink. Maybe it is your birthday, or the weekend, or you just got home from work. The bottom line is we don't need alcohol to survive. However, drinking is fun if done recreationally, but it can lead to some nasty repercussions. Be aware that by drinking to get drunk you are hurting yourself and your well-being. But don't let that stop you from having a great time!

Always enjoy yourself. If you really loved life, you wouldn't need alcohol.

DAY 78
GOAL CHECK #2

"Obstacles are those frightful things you see when you take your eyes off your goal."

Henry Ford

How are your goals coming along? It is now time to start visualizing your goals if you have not already done so. Take a few moments to sit in quiet stillness and picture your goal as if it were happening right now. Feel the sensations in being in that moment of accomplishment. What are the sounds? The images? The smells? The more vivid the picture, the better. For example, if your goal is to lose twenty-five pounds, picture yourself having already lost the weight.

Take a few moments today and every day to visualize your goals. This will propel you forward on your road to greatness.

Day 79
Time

"The only reason for time is so that everything does not happen at once."

Albert Einstein

Time is man-made. There is no such thing as time. The best way to describe it is this: if you were to go into outer space, you would see that the sun never rises or sets. The vastness of space puts everything into perspective. Time creates a great deal of stress in our lives. When you are feeling rushed or late, the body tenses up and becomes irritable. However, time is necessary to live in our world. Without time we would not be able to make appointments and live our lives with a sense of order. Time is a very useful tool, but it does not exist.

Whenever you feel the pressure of time, try to remember that it is a figment of your imagination. Take some deep breaths.

Day 80
Exaggeration

"There are people so addicted to exaggeration they can't tell the truth without lying."

Josh Billings

Often we exaggerate a certain event or situation. We want to make a point or prove something to somebody. However, when you exaggerate you are only proving something to yourself. You are proving that what happened in reality was not as extravagant as you had thought. In fact, the situation doesn't really mean anything at all. You are just building it up in your own mind and giving it life by talking about it. There is no need to exaggerate. Your life is what it is, and you are only hurting yourself by not living up to your own expectations.

Be happy with what you have accomplished. You were given your reality for a reason. There is no need to make up a false one.

Day 81
Spring

"Spring is nature's way of saying, 'Let's party!'"

Robin Williams

Spring is a time of new beginnings. As the long winter comes to an end, it's great to have the opportunity to move forward into a new season. Spring is the season of life. The days get longer and the ground thaws, giving birth to new life. It is exciting to experience the changes all around. During this period of time, changes are happening not only externally but also internally. You are part of a life cycle that has once again returned to its beginning stages.

Take a few moments to visit nature today. Smell the fragrances and enjoy the ever-changing cycle of life.

Phase II—Insight

Teachings of the I Ching

Day 82
I Ching

"The inner eye does not see upon command."

J.K. Rowling

The I Ching is a book of divination. Its text dates as far back as the third century BC. The ancient Chinese believed there are sixty-four different types of situations in life, which co-relate to nature's elements. Each situation can be looked at in six different ways. There is always a lesson to be learned. Each situation is called a gua, and the elements of the gua can be either yin or yang. The ancient Chinese recognized that there is no good or bad; however, we do live in a world of opposites. Instead, there is only energy consisting of dark and light, and when put in specific orders they are given significant meaning.

Reflect on how life has changed thus far since the beginning of your journey to self-realization. A foundation of positivity has been built.

Day 83
The Upper Canon

"Look deep into nature, and then you will understand everything better."

Albert Einstein

The next thirty days will deal with the teachings of the upper canon from the I Ching. All thirty lessons encompass the power of heaven with the responsive power of earth. We see darkness and the moon as a source of energy that gives way to the brightness of the sun and the light of day. These teachings deal with our inner being and the role of nature. Our relationship with Mother Nature is vital to our existence and is crucial in the process of awakening our inner being from unconsciousness.

Can you feel our interconnectedness with all things? This next phase will open your body, mind, and soul to new possibilities and ways of thought. Be open and experience change within yourself.

Day 84
Initiating

"Without change there is no innovation, creativity, or incentive for improvement. Those who initiate change will have a better opportunity to manage the change that is inevitable."

William Pollard

Initiating is the act of being creative. All creative energy comes from infinite source. The process of initiating is heaven above, heaven below; pure yang, or white light. The image of creating is the sun rising and radiating its energy onto the earth. One who is initiating is healthy, firm, strong, and full of energy. When we are creative and have ideas, we are in contact with pure yang energy. This is why it is so important to be creative. Express yourself through right-brain activity, such as playing music, painting, writing, drawing, etc.

Enjoy the process of creating. Use your talents as much as possible. Through creativity you will feel full of energy and experience joy beyond belief.

Day 85
Responding

"Respond intelligently even to unintelligent treatment."

Lao Tzu

Responding is pure yin energy. It is earth above and earth below. Initiating and responding act together as an introduction to all sixty-four gua. Responding represents our relationship with Mother Earth. To be submissive is to receive the energy of the world. When the light of initiating (an idea) hits the earth (you), your first act should be to submit fully to the energy and feeling of the whole. The light shines on the darkness of the world with pure yang energy, and the earth responds with its opposite, yin. To be of pure yin is to be the most responsive, devoted, and humble.

When you have an idea, are you responsive to it? Do you allow yourself to feel the pureness of energy and submit fully?

Day 86
Beginning

"Motivation is what gets you started. Habit is what keeps you going."

Jim Rohn

Beginning is cloud above, thunder below. The image of beginning can be best related to a seedling. When first born, the sprout has to penetrate the soil. This is a difficult task, especially if the ground is hard. New beginnings are difficult. Once heaven and earth were created, myriad beings followed. To start something new is like being a newborn baby. It is difficult at first, but you should always know that abundance is yours. Life is an illusion and is therefore not difficult. We are beings of pure energy. We must all start somewhere.

Think of a time when you started something new. How difficult was the beginning compared to the middle and the end?

Day 87
Childhood

"There is a garden in every childhood, an enchanted place where colors are brighter, the air softer, and the morning more fragrant than ever again."

Elizabeth Lawrence

The ancient Chinese realized that children are brilliant; however, they do not possess the wisdom to uncover their genius. A child is ignorant and innocent and thus needs education. We experience childhood many times in our life—when we start a new career, play a new game or sport, or when we know little about a topic. The image of childhood is mountain above water. This is an image of a stream of water flowing out of a mountain. The knowledge flows out easily; however, over time the water accumulates moss and sediment. This is why it is important to educate the child.

Is there something you would like to learn? There is always something you do not know. It is never too late to learn. In fact, the day you stop learning is the day the sediment forms on your stream of water.

DAY 88
NEEDING

"Earth provides enough to satisfy every man's need, but not every man's greed"

Mahatma Gandhi

We all require proper nourishment for a healthy body and mind. When a farmer plants his crops he never worries about sunshine, air, or earth, because they are abundant. However, rain is necessary to water the crops. The symbol of this gua is cloud above, heaven below. This is an image of clouds forming above the earth, which indicates it is about to rain. One in this position requires patience because it is a time of waiting. We experience many instances of waiting in life. To realize this requires faith that what has been sown will be reaped.

Have you planted your crops? Are you waiting patiently for something to happen? Or are you at a loss because the thing you want has not happened yet?

Day 89
Contention

"It's our tendency to approach every problem as if it were a fight between two sides."

Deborah Tannen

Another translation for *contention* is conflict. After a time of needing and searching for food, contention follows. The symbol is heaven rising upward and water flowing downward. The water represents a mean intention, while heaven signifies a strong, firm character. No perfect result can ever arise from contention or conflict. This is why it is always best to search for middle ground when we are in conflict. When differences arise within people, we have a tendency to be selfish and egotistical.

When dealing with conflict always look for a middle ground. Come to terms with both sides equally, and there will be good fortune.

Day 90
Multitude

"No man, for any considerable period, can wear one face to himself and another to the multitude, without finally getting bewildered as to which one is true."

Nathaniel Hawthorne

Multitude is the teaching of people coming together. Usually people come together in large groups for a cause. The ancient Chinese make reference to an army. The symbolism is earth above, water below. After contention (conflict), a multitude follows (army). This is the law of attraction at work. Whatever you focus on comes to you in abundance. If it is conflict you want, then that is what you shall have. If you seek harmony and are steadfast and firm, you will have a multitude of love and kindness. Through multitude you can bring peace to the world.

Be careful what you intend and think. Your power is far greater than you can ever imagine. Always be loving and positive in your thoughts and actions.

DAY 91
UNION

"The three ingredients of a successful union between two ... humor, commitment & undying love."

Bill Cosby

Water above, earth below is the inverse of multitude. It suggests that when water flows on the earth the ground softens. There is a union. After multitude, the people seek peace and harmony. Communities work together toward one goal. If their goals are in alignment with their purpose, and the people are coming together and working in unison with each other, then there is good fortune. To be successful you need the cooperation of other people.

Look around and see the union between groups of people. We create relationships and forward-thinking movements. How do your actions contribute to a greater good?

Day 92
Little Accumulation

"If you wrote a page per day, in one year you would have a three-hundred-and-sixty-five-page novel."

Jack Canfield

Little accumulation is to acquire nourishment. When people are united, there comes a point when nothing seems to happen. It's like looking in the sky and seeing storm clouds, but there is no rain. The symbol is wind above, heaven below. Wise people realize there is always a need to gather strength. Eventually it will rain. When the time comes you must be strong. Little accumulation is about winning the little battles—making gains in the small areas of your life. Little things add up.

Think about the daily accomplishments you have made to get to where you are today. Little accumulation is the key to great success.

Day 93
Fulfillment

"The only thing that will stop you from fulfilling your dream is you."

Tom Bradley

The process of fulfillment begins with action. After little accumulation and building up strength, fulfillment follows. The symbol of this gua is heaven above, lake below. Heaven represents strength and energy, while lake means to be gentle. A wise person will always attain fulfillment through moral conduct. Once you are well prepared the time will come to take what is rightfully yours. You must be firm and strong and realize you deserve what is coming. Have faith.

Believing in yourself is one of the greatest lessons we can learn. Believe in abundance and a higher power. Know it exists. Do you have faith?

Day 94
Advance

"Winners make a habit of manufacturing their own positive expectations in advance of the event."

Brian Tracy

Advance is an image of earth above, heaven below, or yin above yang. This seems to be the opposite of what we expect in reality. We always think of heaven moving upward from the earth. Advance is a time when greatness comes to earth. After fulfillment and attaining a goal, advance follows. This means to be joyful and happy—to experience bliss in all its forms. Advance is a time of rest and reflection, to see the beauty around you and realize you are one with all that is. You have accomplished greatness because you are a part of the infinite.

Relax. Take time to recognize the amazing life with which we live. We are abundant and perfect.

DAY 95
HINDRANCE

"The man who gives up accomplishes nothing and is only a hindrance. The man who does not give up can move mountains."

Ernest Hello

Hindrance is the inverse of advance. This gua is heaven above earth, signifying that the two are moving away from each other. A time of hindrance is a time of misfortune. However, it is important to understand that hindrance is a law of nature. A person cannot be successful all the time. This is why it is important to not get attached to success. There will always be a point where one loses or creates misfortune. A time of hindrance is not necessarily a bad thing. It gives you the chance to be grateful for what you already have.

In a time of misfortune or bad luck, realize there is no such thing as luck at all. All situations are caused in part by you. In times of adversity, be appreciative for what you have.

Day 96
Seeking Harmony

"People in the same boat help each other, sharing in weal and woe."

Ancient Chinese Maxim

Seeking harmony means to work in union with other people. After a time of hindrance or tough times, seeking harmony amongst people follows. The wise person understands that people have different personalities. When bringing people together, he or she must treat the people according to their personalities to ultimately gain insight on common ground. A wise person seeking harmony will forgo the tiny issues to resolve the big problems in order to obtain harmony.

We are all equal. Seek harmony in this way. There is no boss when all are united, with a common goal.

Day 97
Great Harvest

"Always do your best. What you plant now, you will harvest later."

Og Mandino

After one seeks harmony amongst the people, a great harvest ensues. The meaning of a great harvest is abundance. If a person works in perfect harmony with his or her surroundings, prosperity will unfold. Both people and Mother Earth are great. When they work together, there is great success and good fortune. When considering your vocation, be sure to create positivity amongst your fellow workers to obtain the right outcome. It is important to recognize there is no such thing as possession. The image of a lunar eclipse is used to illustrate the absence of the moon, creating darkness in the world. All possessions are eventually taken away, so it is wrong to seek out others' wealth. There is plenty of abundance for everyone.

Utilize your talents to create your own wealth and abundance in the world. Allow your hobbies to become your monetary pleasures.

Day 98
Humbleness

"Only the humble are capable of commanding."

Lao Tzu

To be humble is one of the greatest virtues we can possess as human beings. Humility takes a lifetime to develop, and its main purpose is to abolish the ego. One achieves greatness and success through humbleness. This selflessness comes from the realization that all talents and successes are of the divine. We were given our special talents and gifts from a higher power. There is no such thing as *I* or *Me*. We are all connected. To be humble is to be balanced.

Great success and outstanding achievements come from hard work, and practice, and patience. One who is humble recognizes this.

Day 99
Delight

"For he that hath, to him shall be given: and he that hath not, from him shall be taken, even that which he hath."

Mark 4:25

When a person has a great harvest and is humble, delight follows. The structure of delight is thunder above, earth below. Thunder represents action, while the earth is submissive. When thunder claps, it can be heard for many miles over the earth. Therefore, when you are happy with your given situation and have obtained your goals, the world will know. Delight comes from humbleness; the two are complementary. One who experiences joy is in the right frame of mind and will be praised for his or her results.

Take delight in others' accomplishments. See the beauty and success around you. Be grateful.

Day 100
Following

"Those who try to lead the people can only do so by following the mob."

Oscar Wilde

We all follow the course of time. Following has significance because it holds a great virtue. To be a great leader, a person would have to be an inspired follower at one point or another. Even as a great leader, one still follows the will of God. In order to follow, you must lead with your heart. Be steadfast and truthful to yourself, and you will find your way. We live a life of following, and as a result create the leadership required to move great mountains. The structure is lake above, thunder below. The water of lake flows with the action of thunder.

Be a great listener and follower, and in return you will be a great leader—not the other way around.

Day 101
Remedying

"Don't find fault, find a remedy."

Henry Ford

The symbol of remedying is three worms in a chalice. It is a sign that the work has been spoiled. Over a long period of time, worms develop and bring about decay. A remedy is needed to cure the sickness. This brings about innovation and new beginnings. The structure is mountain above, wind below. The mountain is strong and firm, but the wind below blows and decays the base of the mountain. The mountain symbolizes your present situation of being stubborn and not seeing the truth. Thus a change is needed because one cannot stand still in this position for very long. When someone is a follower, he or she must be sure to follow the right leader.

Always follow your heart and dreams. If a change is needed to attain your goals, do it. Start now.

Day 102
Approaching

"Difficulties increase the nearer we approach the goal."

Johann Wolfgang

After many changes have been made, there is an arrival of great good fortune. A time of approaching follows a remedy because the cure is at hand. A time of approaching requires great leadership. It is the knowledge that one is on the right path and the outcome will be prosperous. A time of approaching requires perseverance and faith. One has made many changes and as a result will experience a great turn of events. The structure is earth above, lake below. This symbolizes standing on higher ground viewing the entire lake. A person sees the progress made and recognizes the great good fortune to come.

Great indeed is the time of change. Blessed are those who follow their true paths to freedom and prosperity. Are you on your path to freedom?

Day 103
Watching

"Work like you don't need the money, love like your heart has never been broken, and dance like no one is watching."

Aurora Greenway

When one experiences greatness, he or she is constantly being watched. It is very important to lead by example. A great leader will always be watched and mimicked. Watching also means that you need to be conscious of your thoughts. You must monitor the thoughts that arise unconsciously as the day's events unfold. The Chinese use a wooden fish to symbolize watching. A fish never closes its eyes and is therefore always aware of its surroundings. Because people are always watching, leaders must be sensitive to their morality and always remain focused.

Practice leading by example by always doing and never telling. Words are meaningless in comparison to action.

Day 104
Eradicating

"One bad apple spoils the whole bunch."

Proverb

After people watch a great leader, they tend to draw closer and come together. However, this coming together brings a closeness that is not always favored. There are times when we experience obstructions. These counterproductive factors can be a person, a job, or even a habit. The wise make the choice to eradicate the obstruction by either letting it go, or punishing him or her fairly. After justice is established, there will be success once again. However, if one does not eradicate the problem, it will only grow and cause disharmony.

Take notice of the problems you encounter. How do you deal with them? Do you see them as obstacles to be overcome?

Day 105
Adorning

"Adorn your speech."

Sam Veda

The structure of this gua is mountain above, fire below. There is a fire at the foot of the mountain, illuminating and adorning its firmness and beauty. After an obstruction is eradicated, compliments go to the righteous follows. It is right to give praise to the people who work hard and do well for the common good. Mountain and fire go hand in hand as the firm and strong complement the bright and beautiful. When people are working together in harmony, adorning is sure to take place. Adorning leads to uplifted spirits and positivity.

Always make known your appreciation for others, especially in work-related activities. Let them know that no good deed goes unnoticed.

DAY 106
FALLING AWAY

"People remain what they are even if their faces fall apart."

Bertolt Brecht

Falling away follows adorning because if the adorned is praised too much, the firm and strong will rely on the soft and weak. The structure is mountain above, earth below. This is an image of a mountain falling to the ground and resting on the soft earth. There is nowhere to go. The significance is the falling away of one's belief in him- or herself. If one discontinues having faith, he or she will rely solely on other people. If you rely completely on other people and neglect your inner awareness, surely you will fall apart.

Always remember that you are special, strong, and abundant. You can achieve anything and become anything.

Day 107
Turning Back

"No matter how far you have come on the wrong road, turn back."

Turkish Proverb

When circumstances have fallen away to the maximum point, turning back begins. This is a sequence of new beginnings. Things can only erode to a certain point before a new starting point is established. This is like the changing of the seasons. Turning back represents the eleventh month of the Chinese calendar. The outer structure is earth, while the inner is thunder. Mother Earth yields to the action of thunder. Therefore a time of turning back is when we move forward without destruction. In world history, upon the defeat of Adolf Hitler most of Germany was left in ruins. It was a time of turning back. Now Germany is once again a strong and prosperous country.

When breaking old habits, there is a time of difficulty. Know that this is a time of learning. Nothing can stop you from achieving success except yourself.

Day 108
Without Falsehood

"Falsehood is cowardice, the truth courage."

Hosea Ballou

To be honest and sincere is the natural state of a person. To be without falsehood is a virtue we all possess, but few cultivate. After falling away and turning back, people are sincere and truthful. The way is clear, and everyone gives a helping hand. To be clear of mind and honest with yourself is the way of heaven. The structure of this gua is heaven above, thunder below. Through the action of thunder, the will of heaven is restored. When one is aligned with the will of heaven, great prosperity will ensue. Great is the time of no faults.

Good intentions and sincerity are a life mission. Be truthful and fulfill your purpose. Your way will be prosperous.

Day 109
Great Accumulation

"Courage is only an accumulation of small steps."

George Konrad

When an individual leads with the heart and is sincere, great accumulation follows. The structure is mountain above, heaven below. This means that during a time of great accumulation, one must be firm and strong like a mountain to obtain the greatness of heaven. When you are sincere and speak from the heart, you will be given great rewards. There is abundance all around, and the law of attraction is always at work. You will be rich with life, love, and material goods by following your passion. Be truthful to yourself, and the rest will follow.

Great indeed is the one who finds his or her purpose. It is sad that in most cases it takes a catastrophic event to change one's ways. Is there something you need to change?

Day 110
Nourishing

"Whatever we plant in our subconscious mind and nourish with repetition and emotion will one day become a reality."

Earl Nightingale

After a time of great accumulation, one must have nourishment. Usually nourishment means food and drink. However, here we are talking about the mind. The structure is mountain above, thunder below. A mountain stands still while thunder moves with action. When we eat, the upper jaw is still while the lower jaw moves and chews the food. When people have attained great accumulation, they must watch not only how they feed themselves, but others as well. You must nourish your people with wisdom and understanding to continue the time of prosperity.

Always take the time to nourish your body, mind, and soul. This means exercise, nutrition, meditation, and contemplation.

DAY 111
GREAT EXCEEDING

"A man's reach should exceed his grasp, or what's a heaven for?"

Robert Browning

Great exceeding is the opposite of nourishing. However, the two interact and are complementary. This is a time of action. When people are well nourished, great exceeding follows. A time of great action cannot be accomplished without proper nourishment. This can be looked at from many angles. We need money, food, drink, shelter, rest, time, and exercise. Without the basic nourishment, one cannot perform to full potential. Always be sure that your needs are being met, along with those of any other people you may encounter. If you have a joint venture, it is vital that everyone's needs are met before forward advancement is to take place.

Always listen to your body. It is wise and knows what it needs. You are spirit living in the body and should take care of your temporary home.

Day 112
Darkness

"I will love the light for it shows me the way, yet I will endure the darkness because it shows me the stars."

Og Mandino

Darkness is the equivalent of a dark pit or a tough situation. The structure is water above, water below. The color of water is blue-black. There is no light. Water is significant because it symbolizes danger such as drowning. However, no matter how bad the situation, it can always be reversed by being truthful to yourself and relying on heart and mind. Darkness is also significant because it is yin energy. We live in a world of opposites. Darkness and light: moon and sun. The moon is bright because of the sun's reflection. When one experiences darkness, it is like being trapped in a pit. Always rely on your inner guidance.

Great exceeding is not always the case in a world of opposites. There will be times of darkness. Always be sure of yourself. Rise above the darkness into the light.

Day 113
Brightness

"We see the brightness of a new page where everything yet can happen."

Rainer Maria Rilke

Brightness is the opposite of darkness. The structure is fire above, fire below. Brightness also means attachment. When darkness has fallen, one finds attachment in others and thus creates brightness and hope. When times are dark, we need to step into the light. This means to shed light on the situation, to look at what is happening from an outside point of view. It is not always easy to see our own situations from an outer perspective. This is why it is important to consult others who are wiser for guidance.

To rise into the light is to seek guidance from inspiring individuals. Be sure to confide in those you trust.

Day 114
The Lower Canon

"After Heaven and Earth have come into existence, there are myriad beings."

I Ching

In the last thirty days we have dealt with the upper canon, the Tao of heaven. We will now look at the lower canon, the Tao of humanity. The next thirty-four days will cover the cycle of human affairs between men and women. Once again yin and yang express in every aspect of life. The influence of the lower canon is present every day we live on Mother Earth. We now delve into natural phenomena and human behavior.

Reflect on your relationships with others. How do the actions of others affect you? We are all interconnected.

Day 115
Mutual Influence

"I love you not because of who you are, but because of who I am when I am with you."

Roy Croft

Mutual influence represents the courtship of a man and a woman. When the two come together willingly and influence each other, there is attraction. This is a good relationship, as both man and woman follow their hearts. The structure is lake above, mountain below. The lake sinks down while the mountain rises upward. The lake is like the woman—soft, gentle, and nurturing. The mountain is like the man—strong, steadfast, and upright. When the two are mutually influenced and come together, it is true love. The man and woman become husband and wife.

Lead with your heart not only in romance, but also in daily endeavors. True love will surround you at all times.

Day 116
Long-Lasting

"Behind every great man there is a great woman."

Meryll Frost

When a man and woman become husband and wife, long-lasting follows. A relationship should never be short-lived. The structure is thunder above, wind below. The man and woman have switched roles. Mutual influence speaks of newlyweds, while long-lasting is about an old married couple. Wind represents the woman being gentle and playing her role in the household. Thunder signifies the man taking action. A long-lasting relationship requires sincerity and selflessness.

In modern society there is often a role reversal between men and women in the home. How is your relationship with your significant other? Is it positive and constructive, or negative and defeating?

Day 117
Retreat

"Nowhere can man find a quieter or more untroubled retreat than in his own soul."

Marcus Aurelius

Things cannot always remain in the same place for long. After long-lasting, retreat follows. The wise person knows when to retreat and gain strength. A time of retreat is a time of creativity. One must stop moving forward in order to reflect and create. When long-lasting occurs, eventually the weak gain too much strength, and therefore the wise must turn back in order to preserve their well-being. The structure is heaven above, mountain below. The greatness of heaven is given to the strong and firm. There is no action to take. One must retreat to seclusion to think and gain insight.

We all need quiet time in our lives. Rest and reflection are mandatory to keep our sanity. No matter how great your situation is, you must always find time for yourself.

Day 118
Great Strength

"Strength does not come from physical capacity. It comes from an indomitable will."

Mahatma Gandhi

After one retreats he or she acquires great strength. The structure is thunder above, heaven below. The action of thunder moves with the strength and greatness of heaven. Strength is not only physical, although it also implies this; it is also mental. Great strength comes from being true to yourself and others. When you have reflected about your goals and aims, you will have the power to carry out your intentions. You can do anything and become anything. However, it is not enough to want. You must think and gather resources. Then put your plan into action with the great strength of heaven.

People are not successful by chance. It takes planning and foresight to acquire the virtue of great strength. Love and be loved. The way is prosperous and smooth.

DAY 119
PROCEEDING FORWARD

"Don't dwell on what went wrong. Instead, focus on what to do next. Spend your energies on moving forward toward finding the answer."

Denis Waitley

The structure is fire above, earth below. Fire signifies the sun. This is an image of the sun rising over the earth. When great strength is accumulated, one cannot remain stagnant for long. Eventually, one will move forward with great strength, nourishment, and wisdom. When someone has the traits of great strength and moves forward with his or her higher purpose, the results are very prosperous and smooth. It is for this reason that it's wise to reflect and wait for the right time to move forward. When your time comes—and it will—the path will be made through ways that cannot be described.

Everyone's path to greatness is different. Yet we all have the same underlying purpose: to be happy. Be who you were meant to be, and enjoy the gift of life.

Day 120
Brilliance Injured

"Know Me to be the eternal seed of all creatures. I am the intelligence of the intelligent, and the brilliance of the brilliant."

Bhagavad Gita

This is the inverse of proceeding forward. The structure is earth above, fire below. When one moves forward, there is always a risk of injury. This is why it is always wise to hide one's brilliance by being gentle and lying low. To show your talents and virtues is to rise above the people, and when this happens, you are at risk with other people's ego. It is for this reason you should always remain gentle and gracious to others without showing off. There is no need to prove your worth to anybody. We are all unified and unique at the same time. There is no such thing as special, because it would mean there is also someone who is not special. To be brilliant is to show compassion.

Show your brilliance of self-worth without boasting or needing. Use your newfound awareness to better the lives of others and abolish your own selfishness.

Day 121
Household

"What is important to a relationship is a harmony of emotional roles and not too great a disparity in the general level of intelligence."

Mirra Komarovsky

Family is a most important virtue of life. When your brilliance is injured, you will surely return home. Men and women must have their proper places within the household. In ancient times the woman would stay at home while the man would work. In modern times this is not always the case, and it does not have to be. However, in order for a household to be efficient and harmonious, everyone must serve his or her role equally. The structure is wind above, fire below. The wind is blowing the warmth of the fire and so creates harmony and peace. One's household should be a place of peace and goodness. Your family is always the most important in all your endeavors.

Appreciate your family and the roles each member serves, be it husband, wife, daughter, or son. Know that each has a specific role, and when that role is met, there is harmony.

Day 122
Diversity

"There never were in the world two opinions alike, no more than two hairs or two grains; the most universal quality is diversity."

Michel de Montaigne

Eventually, sons and daughters grow up, get married, and move out. Diversity signifies the interests of the offspring seeking outside relationships and having different visions. After household, diversity will follow. The structure is fire above, lake below. A fire moves upward while a lake moves down into the earth. This is a symbol of the two daughters going in separate directions, each living her life in the way she wishes. This cannot be avoided, nor should it be. In a harmonious household diversity is sure to arise and should be embraced. The way will be prosperous. Part of a parent's obligation is to let go of his or her children and allow them to live their own lives. If they were raised in the proper manner, they will make the right choices.

You cannot change other people; you can only change yourself. In changing yourself you change those around you. Be a good listener and allow people's lives to take on lives of their own. There is no need to control. To do so only creates stress.

Day 123
Hardship

"Sorrow happens, hardship happens, the hell with it, who never knew the price of happiness, will not be happy."

Yevgeny Yevtushenko

When there is a misunderstanding in a household that was created from diversity, hardship arises. A period of hardship is a time when one must turn inward for guidance. This does not mean to give up. In fact, we all experience hardship. The greater the goal to achieve, the greater the hardship to endure. The structure is water above, mountain below. Climbing mountains and crossing rivers are not easy. When times are tough, we must be patient. When you are diverse and attempt to accomplish something not many have done, the way is not clearly defined. It does not mean to stop. It means to reflect. Great is your reward for following your heart.

The pioneers and leaders of our time all had to undergo hardship in order to succeed. Hardship helps us appreciate our goals when they come to fruition.

Day 124
Relief

"Your career is like a crack in a foundation. It is unpredictable and will go in all directions."

Gil Moore

The structure of relief is thunder above, rain below. This is the image of a thunderstorm. It is very chaotic and temporary. Hardship cannot last forever. Relief is like the rain washing away dirt from the skin. The skin is temporarily clean. However, if a person continues in the same behaviors, the skin will be dirty once more. Relief is a time when one should rest and reflect. It is like when your shoulders are tense with stress and you notice you are shrugging. When you relax the shoulders, you experience relief. Unaware, however, you will shrug your shoulders again and again. Relief is a time to be aware. Notice your feelings and how your body responds. Be true to yourself.

You will always experience times of turbulence on your journey. Your focus determines your reality.

Day 125
Decreasing

"A career is a series of ups and downs, of comebacks."

Steve Guttenberg

When relieving is done for too long, surely decreasing will follow. A time of decrease happens naturally when one neglects a certain aspect of his or her life. The structure is mountain above, lake below. The mountain rises as the lake at the foot of the mountain decreases. The water from the lake evaporates into the air and disperses at the top of the mountain. It is for this reason that a sage employs minions to perform mundane tasks. Surely one person cannot keep up with all the demands of any given occupation unless he or she has people to take care of the little things. There are only so many hours in the day, and tasks must be delegated.

Decreasing happens through neglect. Be sure to focus your efforts on what is important. All other tasks can be given to others.

Day 126
Increasing

"Thoughts become things. If you see it in your mind, you will hold it in your hands."

Bob Proctor

Increasing is the opposite of decreasing. The two relate to each other. When decreasing seizes, increasing begins. The structure is wind above, thunder below. When wind and thunder combine, they double in power. When a wise person finds a fault in him- or herself, he or she changes it as quickly as the wind, with the action of thunder. We are forever in times of increase and decrease in all areas of life. When something is increasing, surely a different aspect of life is decreasing. When food is consumed, the plate becomes empty while the stomach is filled. Increasing and decreasing are natural processes and are neither good nor bad. To increase any part of life, one must put focus and action on it. To obtain financial wealth, one must be aware of money and accept it into his or her life.

You cannot have ups without downs. This is a world of opposites. Remember this during your down times.

Day 127
Eliminating

"Eliminating what is not wanted or needed is profitable in itself."

Phillip Crosby

One must eliminate all negative forces to be supreme in nature. When something has increased too much, eliminating follows. With proper focus the wise person eliminates all that is unnecessary from his or her life. The structure is lake above, heaven below. The water in the clouds will rain on the greatness of the earth. This signifies the tension within human society. It is vital to spread the good word and to speak from the heart. It is through righteous example that inferiority will subside. We are all equal and should not have to succumb to elimination and poverty.

There is abundance all around. Great is the Way of natural flow and oneness. Live in peace and spread goodwill.

Day 128
Encountering

"We may encounter many defeats but we must not be defeated."

Maya Angelou

Once you have eliminated the negative forces in your life, surely you will encounter something new. To encounter is to proceed with caution. The structure is heaven above, wind below. Wind blows under all beneath heaven. When one eliminates negative forces, there are going to be some unexpected residual outcomes to deal with before one can proceed. It is like quitting a bad habit. Take smoking, for instance. If you have been a smoker for many years and decide to quit cold turkey, at first everything might seem fine. Then you may get sick as your body dispels all the toxins from the years of abuse. Encountering is a warning about change. It must be done swiftly and firmly. Once the decision is made, one cannot go back.

Be firm, strong, and honest with yourself. Prepare mentally before embarking on dispelling the negative. Only in this way will you be successful.

Day 129
Bringing Together

"We bring together the best ideas—turning the meetings of our top managers into intellectual orgies."

Jack Welch

Bringing together, after encountering and dealing with negative forces, results in power. When all negative forces are put to rest, the wise and powerful are able to lead a nation. The structure is lake above, earth below. The water of the lake is abundant on the soil of the earth. Nothing can stop the bringing together of positive energy, as it is exponentially greater than negative force. Bringing together can also be thought of in terms of the law of attraction. When positive thoughts are your way of thinking, eventually you will bring forth your true nature. You will cultivate your true talents and excel at your calling.

Positivity is instrumental in bringing together like-minded individuals. Goals are accomplished through faith and belief.

Day 130
Growing Upward

"All of the top achievers I know are lifelong learners. If they're not learning, they're not growing."

Denis Waitley

Growing upward can be seen as a tree breaking through the earth. Hence the structure earth above, wood below. Weeds take a short period to grow and rise. They are easily plucked and abolished. However, a tree has deep roots that take time to grow into the earth. When this process is complete, the tree grows upward. The way is unobstructed. The tree is free to grow upward without any hindrance and is strong and firm. The life span of a tree is long, and its process is smooth and effortless. This is the Way of the Tao. To live effortlessly in accordance with your true nature is to be pure of heart. When bringing together has come about from purity and divinity, growing upward follows.

When everything you do is from the love of your heart, life is effortless. Enjoy your livelihood and goodwill toward others. It is your true nature.

Day 131
Exhausting

"With every unfortunate circumstance there is always the seed of a greater or equivalent benefit."

Napoleon Hill

In the process of growing upward, if one does not rest and rejuvenate, exhausting will follow. The symbolism is a tree growing in an enclosed area. Eventually, the tree will grow to its limit yet still continue to try to grow. It is in this way the energy will be depleted. The structure is lake above, water below. All the water from the lake has been drained, and the lake is now empty. To be in this situation is unfavorable. Life seems daunting and unfortunate. It seems like a series of bad events that will never end. We all experience unpleasant circumstances. However, no matter what the situation there is always hope. It is not about the situation. It is about your point of view.

Oftentimes exhaustion comes in the form of sickness. We overwork ourselves until the body gives signs of needing to slow down.

Day 132
Replenishing

"He that can take rest is greater than he that can take cities."

Benjamin Franklin

When one is exhausted, there is a need for replenishment. The structure is water above, wood below. This symbolizes a well containing water for the people. A well is an inexhaustible resource that provides replenishment day after day. To gain strength, one must realize he or she is the same as everybody else. We all need water to survive. We all need love, nourishment, rest, and exercise. This way of life plays no favorites. To overwork does not mean better results. It means the end of growing upward. In daily life you must pace yourself. Live in accordance with your true nature.

Be happy now. Experience the accomplishments attained on a daily basis as opposed to waiting for the success that seems to never come.

Day 133
Abolishing the Old

"In order to practice meditation, first clean your room."

Dalai Lama

When a well has been used for an extended period of time, dirt accumulates at the bottom. One must clean out the bottom of the well to once again obtain pure drinking water. The structure is lake above, fire below. Two elements opposite each other, water puts out fire, and fire dries up water. Fire and water represent two daughters who have different points of view. The two try to change each other yet refuse to change themselves. To abolish the old, one can change only him- or herself. In doing so the old is abolished, which leaves room for purity and cleansing.

Take notice of how people come and go in your life. New friends and partners indicate change.

Day 134
Establishing the New

"Decide what you want, decide what you are willing to exchange for it. Establish your priorities and go to work."

H. L. Hunt

Great is the time of establishing the new. The structure is fire above, wood below. The wood feeds the fire and is an image of cooking. When you are well prepared and are ready to cook, you can make a feast. It is exciting as the food cooks with all the new fragrances and anticipation. Establishing the new takes wisdom and foresight. One must be able to see the direction to take and the action necessary to get to the destination. In ancient times, establishing the new was seen as a ruler coming into power. A great ceremony would take place with sacrificial offerings given to heaven to nourish the ruler's wisdom and virtue.

In order to cultivate your true purpose, you must be ready. First abolish the old. This means bad habits and negative thoughts. Next comes a time of establishing the new.

Day 135
Taking Action

"The greatest happiness is to transform one's feelings into action."

Madame de Stael

Thunder above, thunder below. Thunder is a symbol for action. The quick strikes of lightning with the roaring sound of thunder. Here the action is doubled in power. The image of an earthquake is used. When an earthquake takes place, it rumbles the earth with no obstruction. People are fearful. As soon as the action is over, they forget about the earthquake and go on with their daily lives. We take action every day in different forms. However, every task eventually comes to an end. We tend to forget about the action as the days and weeks go by. When fear takes over the mind of the people, the wise examine their own faults. In some way, every action and non-action is a result of your own well-being, whether pleasant or unpleasant.

Only take action when absolutely necessary. It is taught by the Tao of heaven to do nothing and let nothing unfold into being and nonbeing.

Day 136
Keeping Still

"One's action ought to come out of an achieved stillness: not to be mere rushing on."

D. H. Lawrence

Keeping still is the opposite of taking action. The structure is mountain above, mountain below. The stillness of the mountain's power is doubled. The virtue of keeping still is not merely about the body, but also of the mind. In Western society we call it meditation—to sit in stillness cultivating calm of mind. To have control over your mind is a discipline that takes practice. It is said that when heaven is about to give a great mission of importance to someone, it first gives him or her discipline of mind. By keeping still and controlling one's thoughts, he or she prepares for the time to perform the will of heaven.

Be aware of your thoughts. You are not what you think. You are the thinker. The ego has no rule over you.

Day 137
Developing Gradually

"The aim of life is self-development. To realize one's nature perfectly—that is what each of us is here for."

Oscar Wilde

Life cannot remain stagnant for very long; therefore, after keeping still, developing gradually follows. The structure is wood above, mountain below. This is symbolic of a tree growing on a mountain. We have talked many times of trees and how they grow strong and firm. This is no exception. The I Ching constantly reminds us that things take time. No matter what the endeavor, one must be patient. If you follow your heart's desire and remain truthful and sincere, eventually supreme good fortune will come to you. It is said that it takes ten years to become an overnight success. Whatever comes quickly leaves quickly. Therefore, developing gradually is the sign of a long journey with a positive ending.

Use your time wisely. What long journey are you embarked on? What little things do you do every day to accomplish your dreams?

Day 138
Marrying Maiden

"I would rather have eyes that cannot see; ears that cannot hear; lips that cannot speak, than a heart that cannot love."

Robert Tizon

The term *marrying maiden* is derived from polygamy. This is when a man has many wives. There are households where the first wife will appoint the second wife and others to follow. Those women appointed have no authority in the household and must answer to the first wife. This status is much like working a job that is not true to one's inner purpose. The situation is not favorable and thus leads to unhappiness. The structure is thunder above, lake below. The action of the storm feeds the lake below. One in this position fails to think for him- or herself because of fear. The basic emotion of fear is what drives so many people to stay unhappy. Not being able to pay the bills is a prime example of a common fear.

Follow your heart. The bills will get paid. Negative thoughts are the ego putting you down.

Day 139
Abundance

"When you are grateful fear disappears and abundance appears."

Anthony Robbins

When one finds a home, abundance follows. Abundance is all around us. We are abundant. This means there are more resources than we could ever require or imagine. There is an infinite supply of love, health, and happiness. Wealth is also infinite. There is no ceiling on the amount of money you can make in a lifetime. There is no shortage of food, water, electricity, or any other resource. To be abundant is to be connected with all that is. However, it is impossible for one person alone to obtain all that is. There simply is too much. This is why the wise share what they have. They know that in reality they have nothing. We are nothing. The mind attracts to it what it thinks about most.

Abundance is all around all the time. Open your eyes. Notice the subtleties in your life and what you have consciously and unconsciously attracted.

Day 140
Traveling

"The world is a book, and those who do not travel read only a page."

Saint Augustine

A time of abundance cannot last very long. One must appreciate all that has been gained and move on swiftly and quickly. Sometimes we experience great success with a person or circumstance. We see the end has approached, yet we hang on to the old ways in the hope of rejuvenating what once was. Moving on is a part of life. To explore new options and change is natural and inevitable. A lot of people fear change and so live in unhappiness because they are comfortable. The structure is fire above, mountain below. The wind blows the fire all around and scatters the ashes all over the mountain. A traveler must be steadfast and strong. The lost always find their way eventually. It is the will of heaven.

It is far better to start a new phase of your life not knowing the outcome than to live in unhappiness for the sake of comfort.

Day 141
Proceeding Humbly

"To be humble to superiors is duty, to equals courtesy, to inferiors nobleness."

Benjamin Franklin

Proceeding humbly is a structure of wind above, wind below. When one follows the way of the wind, he or she proceeds humbly forward. The wind is like the changing of the times. The traveler realizes that every new day is a new opportunity. Even though there may not be a place to stay for one particular evening, that does not mean it will be the same the next night. In this way the traveler is humble. Backpacking through Europe on a limited budget is a great way to learn this lesson. You meet all kinds of people who are willing to help, and others who take advantage. It is always best to follow the flow of nature in all endeavors.

Follow the signs as to your next moves in whatever calling you are involved. Be open to new possibilities and suggestions.

Day 142
Joyful

"Who is the happiest of men? He who values the merits of others, and in their pleasure takes joy."

Johann Wolfgang von Goethe

When you have proceeded humbly with a gentle nature, joyfulness follows. To be joyful means to speak with happiness and to give and receive. Every day, you give and receive—whether you teach, provide a service, give a gift, offer your time, help someone, ask for help, etc. These are normal daily occurrences and are not to be overlooked. Often giving and receiving are taken for granted. The structure is lake above, lake below. When the two lakes come together, they symbolize an abundance of replenishment or food. Lake means a person with a joyful personality with great inner strength. When the two are combined, there is a great person with marvelous intentions.

Be a great giver and receiver. Feel the joy of both actions and know that one cannot take place without the other.

Day 143
Dispersing

"Ignorance can only be dispersed by knowledge; selfishness by love."

James Allen

The structure is wind above, water below. This is symbolic of ice breaking away and melting. After joyfulness, dispersing follows as one must use the joyous energy acquired to disperse and grow. We are forever growing, learning, and evolving. Joy is a temporary state in this lifetime just like everything else. When the feeling subsides, we must achieve new goals and grow further. Life is a process. It is a cycle of beginnings and endings. To disperse is to deploy and develop. In ancient times a leader would send out his troops to gain more ground and discover new land. In business you can see this as new products become available and promoted. New job positions opening as a company expands. New opportunities as people grow and learn.

Dispersing takes time and is necessary. We are a growing species that is forever learning. To disperse our energies is to gain. However, be sure to not spread yourself too thin.

Day 144
Restricting

"Things which restrict the common are to be interpreted rigidly."

Latin Proverb

A time of restricting is to hold back on expenses. The structure is water above, lake below. Water flows into a lake, but only to a certain point. If too much water flows into the lake, it will overflow and flood. This image means to not overspend or spread too thin. After dispersing, restricting follows. It is a necessary process to disperse, but one must know the limits. If you disperse too much, you will only lose energy. Energy can be time, money, resources, etc. Restricting is important because it means to know your boundaries. When planning ahead, you will know how much money can be spent, or how much time something should take. Restricting takes diligence and foresight. Anyone can disperse, but knowing when to restrict takes discipline.

Before starting any new venture, make sure you have a plan. This way, when you disperse your energy, you will know when to hold back. In this way your ego will not take over.

Day 145
Innermost Sincerity

"Sincerity is the way to heaven."

Confucius

Sincerity comes from the heart. It cannot be bought. It must be earned and established. After restriction, innermost sincerity follows as boundaries are abided. The structure is wind above, lake below. The energy of the wind fills the empty space over the vastness of the lake. Wind cannot be seen, yet it is felt. Sincerity is felt from the heart. To be sincere brings about trustworthiness, reliability, confidence, honesty, and many other great attributes. Innermost sincerity is a lifelong process that takes development and diligence. True sincerity takes humility, yielding when faced with contradiction, and being steadfast and upright in the face of adversity. One with innermost sincerity is a leader who is in touch with his or her inner being.

Be true to yourself first. The rest will follow. Your ego will make all kinds of excuses. You are not your things. You are divine and pure. You are innermost sincerity.

Day 146
Little Exceeding

"Real education should educate us out of self into something far finer; into a selflessness which links us with all humanity."

Lady Nancy Astor

When innermost sincerity is put into practice, little exceeding is accomplished. This is a time when everything from the whole is divided into little parts. It is the process of being sincere. When we look at ourselves, we must not look at the entire self, but at all the little parts that make the self. Our life is broken into segments. A day will consist of many small habits and actions that, over time, amount to who we have become. For instance, it takes about five minutes to smoke a cigarette. That five minutes is a segment of your day that can be repeated over and over again. This then becomes a habit that affects your life. Having innermost sincerity requires you to objectively look at how you are treating your body and mind. You will never be able to help others until you help yourself. The structure is thunder above, mountain below. The action of thunder is blocked by the still mountain. Take action on yourself, and the outer world will reflect what is inside of you.

We all have unique abilities and are living for a reason. Help yourself so that we can all benefit from your well-being.

Day 147
Already Fulfilled

"A leader is best when people barely know he exists; when his work is done, his aim fulfilled, they will say: we did it ourselves."

Lao Tzu

Already fulfilled indicates a perfect situation. The structure is water above, fire below. The water is boiled by the upward heat of fire. When we are in this position, our goals have been attained. It is a place of peace and harmony. When little exceeding has come time and time again, eventually the end result will follow. However, we must realize that no situation is ever perfect. When we attain our goals, we must be weary of stagnation. Perfection cannot remain consistent for long, as life is all about beginnings and endings. Being already fulfilled is a climax. After the height has been achieved, it comes time to descend downward. While we are in this state, we must not lose focus and drive. Proceed cautiously in order to preserve the heightened situation.

We all experience highs and lows. During a time of balance it is important to stay focused. Remember you deserve what has come to you, yet at the same time appreciate all that is.

Day 148
Not Yet Fulfilled

"Life will give you whatever experience is most helpful for the evolution of your consciousness."

Eckhart Tolle

This is the final gua in the I Ching. It is fitting that it be the last, as it signifies a new beginning and ending. Already fulfilled is a warning that perfection and completion cannot last long. The structure is fire above, water below. Fire moves upward away from the water, which moves downward. This indicates a difficult situation; yet there is balance. With every ending there is a beginning. Our lives are forever changing and evolving. We must embrace change as a natural process. Our bodies change all the time. On a daily basis millions of cells die while new cells form. Within a short couple of years, our entire body has changed its complete cellular makeup. We forever grow and learn.

Many are unwilling to change. This is unfortunate, because we are beings of change from moment to moment. Allow yourself the freedom to learn and grow.

Phase III
Growth and Development
Lifestyle, Choices, Feelings, and Healing

Day 149
I

"All the knowledge I possess, everyone else can acquire, but my heart is all my own."

Johann Wolfgang von Goethe

I, me, my—they do not exist. It is only an illusion. Yes, we were given a rare gift. Yes, we are here for a purpose. Yes, every one of us is different and unique. However, there is no such thing as I. What makes you? Is it your clothes? How about your car, your vocation, social status, wealth, knowledge, power? None of these exist. So what is I, me, or my? It is life.

Enjoy your gift. Enjoy your life. Be happy that nothing makes who you are. You are nothing's own doing; all the rest is ego.

Day 150
Goal Check #3

"If you don't know where you are going, you will probably end up somewhere else."

Lawrence J. Peter

We are a lot further into the year now, and a lot has been talked about. Look at the goals you identified at the beginning of the year. Are they still what you want? Were they really your heart's desire, or is there something more? Do you find a shift has taken place? Reassess your goals. Consider them deeply and write what you really desire. What will ultimately make you happy? It is different for everyone, and nothing should be overlooked. Do your best. You are more important than you know.

Take five minutes right now to reexamine and rewrite what will truly make you happy.

Day 151
Wants

"There are only two tragedies in life: one is not getting what one wants, and the other is getting it."

Oscar Wilde

What is a want? Why do we desire things? As soon as we acquire what we want, our attention turns to something new that we want. This is ego. It is important to know that a want is different from a need. We need to be well nourished and well rested, and to have the right amount of exercise. For these necessities there are expenses. However, after our needs are met, desires follow. We want more, or so it seems. More will never make us happy. Association with material possessions is one of the main causes of human dysfunction. Advertising agencies know this and so feed the ego. They give you images of how perfect your life will be by using their products or services.

Look around your living space. How many unneeded material possessions do you own? How did this come to be? Would you be any less of who you are without these things?

Day 152
Anniversaries

"A wedding anniversary is the celebration of love, trust, partnership, tolerance and tenacity. The order varies for any given year."

Paul Sweeney

Anniversaries are beautiful. They signify a union between two people, a bond that is very special and everlasting. In this day and age many people are divorced. How is this so? We all change, there is no doubt. However, a lot of people change for the worse. Their minds take over their ways of life, and as a result, they become unhappy. People become bored with their stagnant existence and end up taking out their stress on their spouses. They eventually realize that the person who once gave them pleasure is now only issuing pain. The truth is, true happiness can be attained only from your inner being. To think a person, place, or thing will provide you with happiness is wrong. Your happiness is your own doing. An anniversary is special because anyone in a long-lasting loving relationship knows this.

Be happy now for all you have, whether you are single or in a relationship. Appreciate all that is, for it was given to you because you deserve it.

Day 153
Human Beings

"Human beings, vegetables, or cosmic dust, we all dance to a mysterious tune, intoned in the distance by an invisible player."

Albert Einstein

As human beings, we are intertwined with two distinct parts. The first is the human aspect of our existence. The human portion consists of "all that is." This means physical reality and thoughts. Everything that can be felt through the senses is the human form. This is the world that is forever changing and evolving. In this part of our awareness lies the ego. The second part of us is the being. The being is the giver of life. This is the underlying awareness of all things and thoughts. You are not the voice in your head; you are the awareness that hears those thoughts. You are not your emotions. Everything that is, and ever was, and ever will be, is a part of you.

You are more beautiful than you can possibly imagine. You are. I am.

Day 154
Ego

"Give up all bad qualities in you, banish the ego and develop the spirit of surrender. You will then experience Bliss."

Sri Sathya Sai Baba

There is a need within us to be accepted and loved. With this comes a false sense of reality. Often people think thoughts about themselves or others that make them right or wrong, good or bad, this or that, etc. The ego is the part of you that thinks it is separate from everything else and is either superior or inferior in some way. This alienation is what causes wars to erupt, arguments to ensue, and negativity to exist. It is not until people forgo their egos that the world will be a place of peace and harmony. Peace and harmony do exist, but not in the ego. When one attaches him- or herself to objects, desires, circumstances, or anything of form, the ego is present. It is for this reason that you are so important.

Only you can save humanity, by becoming aware of your ego. You must dissolve the notion that you are separate.

Day 155
Paranoia

"I envy paranoids; they actually feel people are paying attention to them."

Susan Sontag

A lot of people live in a state of insurmountable fear. Where does this fear come from? It is an extreme case of the identification with form. The I or me has completely attached itself to situations and circumstances. The person is in a thought loop that is triggered either by past events or by fictitious current circumstances. This lack of presence has created a person who is completely unaware of his or her own present self. The mind has taken over with an exhausting constant stream of negative thoughts that leave the body tired and sick. The emotions that accompany this paranoia are fear, doubt, worry, and blame. A person in this situation never realizes that he or she is not the thoughts, but rather the awareness that hears them. Until they can become aware of presence, they will forever be at the mercy of the ego.

You probably know someone who is paranoid, or just negative. This is not who they are. They only associate themselves with pain.

Day 156
Faulty Association

"Don't waste your time on jealousy. Sometimes you're ahead and sometimes you're behind. The race is long and, in the end, it's only with yourself."

Baz Luhrmann

With fear, blame, worry, doubt, right or wrong, is a sense of who we perceive ourselves to be. If you are right, it means the other person is wrong. You have made yourself better than the other person. It's just like if you were to say something like, "Can you believe Bob? How could he do such a thing? Doesn't he care about other people?" Indirectly you have made yourself better than Bob, because you have stated how bad he is for doing what he did. You are now above Bob. But this cannot be further from the truth. We are neither superior nor inferior to anyone. We are all equal. How can a person who has billions of dollars be equal to a homeless person? It's simple—there is no such thing as money. There is only an awareness of abundance and an illusion of wealth.

Drama helps no one. Its only function is to feed the ego. Be aware that we are all equal at all times.

Day 157
Celebrities

"I've grown certain that the root of all fear is that we've been forced to deny who we are."

Frances Moore Lappe

Why is it that we hold people to be idols or celebrities? They are no different than you or anyone else. As a matter of fact, most celebrities become famous for an image that is very far removed from who they really are. Take for instance actors who are famous. They spend their entire careers acting like somebody they are not. Yet we feel a certain attachment and praise them as if it were their identity. Their roles touched our lives, and so we feel a connection with them. Just because someone has a vocation that is on television or in movies does not make him or her more significant than, say, a trash collector. In fact, some common vocations are more important than an actor's, yet little recognition is given to these kinds of people.

This is just one example of how the collective human consciousness has evolved into false idolism. Know that everyone is equal.

DAY 158
SIGNIFICANCE

"Use your precious moments to live life fully every single second of every single day."

Marcia Wieder

Sometimes we think that certain circumstances or what someone said or did holds major significance in our lives. The truth is, something is significant only if you acknowledge it as such. Everything simply is. The experiences you encounter in every waking moment are all equally important. We have only one timeless moment, and that is right now. Our now moment is the most significant and is all we truly have. You may think another moment holds more value, like when you met someone or read something that struck you as inspirational. However, every moment is equal. The only difference is how we perceive the moment.

How do you recognize this moment? Are you at peace with your reality? Do you believe that you deserve this moment and that it is significant because you are experiencing it?

Day 159
Detachment

"This too shall pass."

Ancient Chinese Proverb

This saying is a fundamental insight into basic human awareness. This is the essence from which we derive. When we are present in the now moment, there is a realization that nothing of form lasts forever. This truth strengthens our inner self, which leads to a detachment from reality. "This too shall pass" can be applied to any aspect of life, be it people, places, things, or situations. The only part of life that lives forever is your inner spirit. Consciousness and awakening is the knowledge that our divine being is an endless fountain of abundance and joy. We are eternal and everlasting. The things of this world are not. Things come and go. Yet so many people identify themselves only with what can be felt through the five primary senses.

When you are aware that your spirit will never die, circumstances hold less weight. Fear vanishes as emptiness surrounds every cell of your being.

DAY 160
RESENTMENT

"Resentment is like taking poison and waiting for the other person to die."

Malachy McCourt

It is very easy to have resentment or hate for someone or something. The ego loves this. When we find fault in someone or we are unhappy with a given situation, there is a feeling of anger, blame, or unease. This leads to unhappiness and resentment. If you have any negative feelings or thoughts, they must be let go. Often people have triggers that can go off spontaneously and lead to an outburst of anger. Following this may be a sense of hatred for other people's fortunes. Maybe even jealousy. This must end, but only you can save yourself from the grip of the mind.

When negative feelings arise, take notice of what you are experiencing. Your resentment is not because of someone else's actions or circumstance. It is your own mind and your own problem.

Day 161
Knowing Right from Wrong

"Take no thought of who is right or wrong or who is better than. Be not for or against."

Bruce Lee

Every human being knows the difference between right and wrong. Within ourselves is a basic human awareness that allows us to know when what we are doing is right or wrong. However, there are still wrong actions taking place every day in the world. Rape, killing, violence, and neglect of others are just some of the wrongs in our society. For some reason these actions are still taking place and are still visibly present in everyday life. Why is this? If deep down inside we all know the difference, why is this still happening? It is because of sickness of the mind, or ego. Those who perform wrongdoing are at the mercy of their own egos and think they are separate from everyone else. The only way to change this is in you. Changing yourself will in effect change those around you.

In order to help the world, you must be aware of your own thoughts and actions. You cannot change someone else, only yourself.

Day 162
Being Right or Wrong

"One of the hardest things in this world is to admit you are wrong. And nothing is more helpful in resolving a situation than its frank admission."

Benjamin Disraeli

Within ourselves is a false sense of identity when we need to be right. Being right means you are making someone else wrong. There are circumstances when factual knowledge is correct. For instance, if you say, "A kilometer is longer than a meter," then you are right. If someone argues that point, they are wrong. However, bragging or boasting is not necessary, and neither is feeling better than that person. Just because someone didn't know something doesn't make them less. We are all equal, remember? Admitting you are wrong is a form of humility and is rejuvenating. It is impossible to know everything. However, to argue about who is right or wrong in a given situation is only ego making attempts to identify itself.

The next time someone presents you with an argument that is totally opposite of your way of thinking, say, "Thank you for your insight. I never thought of it like that." And move on. If you know he or she is wrong, simply say, "I think you should look into that." And end it there.

Day 163
Fish

"Many men go fishing all of their lives without knowing it is not fish they are after."

Henry David Thoreau

Fish are interesting creatures. They swim and breathe under water, yet they are unaware that water exists. They are completely content with their ways of life and do not desire to be more or less. Schools of fish thrive when they are together in large numbers moving elegantly through water, as if they were one entity. Other fish stay very still and rarely move at all. The life of a fish is simple. There is no vocation, no destination or goal to accomplish. They simply are.

We can learn a great deal from fish. Watch them swim mindlessly.

Day 164
Garbage

"People say I'm extravagant because I want to be surrounded by beauty. But tell me, who wants to be surrounded by garbage?"

Imelda Marcos

Picture a beautiful lake surrounded by nature. Trees show signs of life as birds chirp on this hot, sunny day. Flowers blossom as the wind gently blows. In the near distance is a recreational park where you hear children playing as families gather and have picnics. As you approach, it becomes more apparent that the land is tainted with garbage. There are plastic bags, coffee cups, cans, bottles, and paper all over the place. The site is filthy with people's leftover goods. They have taken advantage of Mother Nature and left their filth behind. Why are we so naive? Why do we throw our waste onto the beautiful earth that we come to enjoy? Can we not see the madness of our actions? To litter is to be selfish. We are wasteful and negligent of others. Who do we expect to clean up after ourselves?

Creating garbage in beautiful places is selfish. It confirms our unconscious ways as a society. Lead by example.

Day 165
Close Friends

"Many people will walk in and out of your life, but only true friends will leave footprints in your heart."

Eleanor Roosevelt

It is interesting to notice over the course of a lifetime how friends come and go. Some people become very close, while others remain only acquaintances. As we learn and grow, like-minded people are attracted while others are repelled. This is the process of change, which is a necessary part of life. It is neither good nor bad when a person comes and goes in your life. It is a natural process. If the person is a true friend for life, you will see him or her again no matter what the circumstance of your discrepancy. Facebook is amazing for this phenomenon. You may have hundreds or thousands of "friends," but how many do you really stay in contact with? It's said that the more friends you have on Facebook, the fewer you have in real life, because you are spending most of your time on the computer. Great friendships take time. If they are really meant to be, then the next time you see each other you will feel as if no time has passed.

One close friend is worth more than one hundred acquaintances.

Day 166
Names

"I confused things with their names: that is belief."

Jean-Paul Sartre

It is interesting how everything has a name. We were all given names at birth. Plants, animals, and things all have names given for the purpose of identification. We also use names to describe things and to put a label to something. Names lead us to develop thoughts and assumptions. When a name is given to something, we automatically picture it in our minds. For instance, if someone says, "Picture a purple elephant," what is your mind's immediate reaction? Well, it forms a picture of a purple elephant, of course. Now what about calling someone a negative name, like loser or jerk. These also paint pictures in our minds. The images may not be as clear as that of a purple elephant, but a stigma or energy is definitely associated with them. Your words create reactions in the body. Positive words create success, harmony, and peace. Negative words create despair, sickness, and fear.

Monitor your words as you go about your day. Notice when you or someone else labels something. They will do this unconsciously, as if they are not a part of it.

Day 167
Planning

"He who fails to plan, plans to fail."

Proverb

Any great accomplishment takes time to plan and implement. There is no such thing as an overnight success. In fact, the people who become popular quickly often say things like, "It took me twelve years to become an overnight success." There is not a single person who has become successful at anything by accident. Planning is crucial, and one must be organized. The further ahead you are able to plan, the greater a success you will accomplish. First, set out a goal to attain. Next, take the time to plan accordingly. Take little steps day by day to accomplish your goal, like sending e-mails, making phone calls, or performing a task. As the days go by, you will get closer and closer to the end result. Be sure to set dates of completion to keep on track.

You have goals. Now use planning to attain them. Planning puts everything into perspective. Put it on a large board if need be.

Day 168
Contacts

"Skill is fine, and genius is splendid, but the right contacts are more valuable than either."

Arthur Conan Doyle Sr.

Whom do you know? This is the key ingredient in becoming successful. Picture yourself needing something. Whom do you turn to first? The people you know, of course. Usually, you will start with those closest to you and work outward from there. The more people you know, the better. You will always need people to help accomplish your dreams. In fact, your dreams always involve people. There is not a single positive human desire that does not involve someone else in some way, shape, or form. A contact can be anybody, depending on what you need. As you become more positive and align yourself with your true purpose, the right people will come into your life.

Whom do you know right now that would be a good person to talk to about achieving your dreams? Contact them.

Day 169
Talking

"There is nothing so annoying as to have two people talking when you're busy interrupting."

Mark Twain

Some people just talk and talk and talk. It never stops. They will just keep going and going until they finally ask you a question. When they ask the question, you get approximately five seconds to speak before they go right back to talking again. It is very hard to be a good listener when someone talks too much. Oftentimes what happens is the mind wanders and thinks about other things while the person goes on and on. You have left the present moment and escaped to other thoughts. Maybe you are plotting an excuse for leaving the one-sided conversation. In any case, when someone talks to you in this manner, it is a time to practice listening. Nothing lasts forever, and neither will their conversation. There is no need for your input. However, these people have a desperate need for someone to listen to them. So do it with all your being and constant awareness.

When talking to people today, try to listen fully with your entire body. Notice the feelings that come over you as they tell their stories.

Day 170
Competition

"Competition is the spice of sports; but if you make spice the whole meal you'll be sick."

George Leonard

What is it about competition? The blood pressure rises as the scenario seemingly becomes more important. Tensions rise and aggression takes over. No matter what form the competition takes—be it sport, games, or creative talents—it is all a mind game. Some people have troubles competing and choke under the pressure, while others succeed greatly. Why? It all comes down to one word: focus. If people choke under pressure, it is because they let their minds dictate the situation, as opposed to just having fun and enjoying themselves. The ones who succeed in competition have a natural love for it and so become better. They focus more intently and become fierce. The key point here is that the only challenge in life is you. Competition is an illusion. The situation has not changed, only your frame of mind. Days, weeks, months, or years later, the situation will have very little importance.

The next time you are in competition of any sort, realize the unimportance of it and just have fun. You will perform a lot better.

Day 171
Tolerance

"The test of courage comes when we are in the minority. The test of tolerance comes when we are in the majority."

Ralph W. Sockman

Do you find yourself tolerating circumstances rather than enjoying them? Sometimes situations are undesirable and may cause feelings of jealousy or aggression. Everything is going well, but then the next moment someone is pushing your buttons and you get upset. You've been good up until that point because you have been tolerating the outer circumstances that have unfolded. They have been tolerated to the point where you lost your temper and created havoc. To tolerate circumstances means you are attached to a person, place, or thing. This usually happens when something you consider to be *yours* is tampered with or violated. However, it is important to realize that nothing in life is really yours. It is all an illusion, one big facade. It is in these moments that clarity can be formed.

When aggression is rising within yourself, take notice that it is because something you have identified with has been threatened; for instance, your girlfriend or boyfriend, your car, or your self-esteem.

Day 172
Mistakes

"A man's errors are his portals of discovery."

James Joyce

Nobody is perfect; everyone makes mistakes. This is a natural process of life. If we did not make mistakes, how would we learn and grow? There is no reason to blame anyone for a mistake. We are all naive. At some point you will do something that you may regret, and your only hope at that point is forgiveness.

Recognize mistakes as learning opportunities not only for others, but also for yourself. Forgive others and be thankful for the chance to learn and grow.

Day 173
Selfishness

"Selfishness is not living as one wishes to live, it is asking others to live as one wishes to live."

Oscar Wilde

Being selfish comes in many forms. The general meaning is to neglect others. When we are selfish, it creates separateness and disorder. In our society selfishness is the number one cause of discontent. It is misleading. What we think is pleasure provides only negative outcomes with temporary gain. Examples of selfishness are vanity, discarding garbage, lacking compassion, creating dramas, abusing drug or alcohol, interrupting, not listening, blaming, being gluttonous, being greedy, etc. The list goes on and on, and all are prevalent in our society. You may ask, How are these actions selfish? Any action is selfish when you do not put others first. Your lack of awareness and presence leaves you in your mind, and not with the world. Your lack of compassion for others puts you before others, and therefore separates you from everyone else. Your excessive drinking or drug taking makes you incoherent and utterly useless in the aid of others.

Not listening to others is not listening to God. Be open to others, and in turn, others will be open to you.

Day 174
Importance

"Nearly everything you do is of no importance, but it is important that you do it."

Mahatma Gandhi

Something is important only if we make it out to be so. Take, for instance, seeing numbers on a clock. Continually seeing numbers on a clock, such as 12:34, is significant only if you think it is. During the course of a day you may look at a clock about one hundred times. So why don't the other times hold meaning for you? What about events such as winning a game, or meeting the right person? These are important only because you make them so. Think about what happens as time passes. The significance of the event diminishes. As the years go by, the fact that you won a baseball game, for instance, holds less meaning. As a matter of fact, nothing in life is really important. Life is meant to be lived, learned, and enjoyed.

The only thing that really is important is your happiness. Your focus determines your reality.

Day 175
Television

"I find television very educating. Every time somebody turns on the set, I go into the other room and read a book."

Groucho Marx

What are the activities you do that make you truly happy? If you say watching television, then you are sadly mistaken. It's amazing how many hours a day the average person sits in front of the television, yet no happiness can ever be obtained from it. You may have temporary satisfaction, but the end result is a feeling of emptiness. The television is meant for entertainment, yet so many use it as a way of life. They spend countless hours wasting away while living vicariously through mundane programming. The drama on a show then becomes a part of their lives. They talk about the characters as if they know them. They are then in disbelief when you haven't watched the same show the night before. Television is a marvelous invention; however, many are addicted to it. Imagine if those precious hours were used for something more productive.

What leisure activities excite you? What can you be doing instead of watching television? To be successful is to change your old bad habits.

Day 176
Discoveries

"Someday, after we have mastered the winds, the waves, the tides, and gravity, we shall harness the energies of love. Then, for the second time in the history of the world, man will have discovered fire."

Teilhard de Chardin

No matter how many new inventions there will be, or how advanced technology becomes, there will always be something new to discover. The greatest accomplishment we can gain from our life journey, is to uncover the mystery of our existence. We are amazing creatures who have yet to discover our limitless potential.

Take notice how inventions have enhanced your daily living. Electricity is a prime example of a great idea that impacts our way of life.

Day 177
Chores

"My second favorite household chore is ironing. My first being hitting my head on the top bunk bed until I faint."

Erma Bombeck

There will always be things that have to be done even if we don't want to do them. We will always have to buy food, clean the house, mow the lawn, etc. Whatever your living conditions, you will always have to do some sort of work to maintain your living space. Even if you have enough money to pay someone to do these chores, there will still be instances when you will have to perform a task you don't particularly like; for example, fix a flat tire, change a diaper, make a meal, or study for school. When you are faced with chores, it is important to accept the moment for what it is. You cannot change what you need to do, but you can change your mind-set. When you are fully present and are giving the chore your full attention, eventually you may come to enjoy the task. Remember, nothing lasts forever.

Appreciate the chores you have to do. You are lucky to have the ability to accomplish them. Everything you do is sacred, whether you believe it or not.

Day 178
Enemies

"It is a man's own mind, not his enemy or foe, that lures him to evil ways."

Buddha

No matter how good a person you are, there will always be enemies. They come in all different forms. Some enemies were once your best friends, but now they apparently hate you. Others just simply don't like something you said or did. Maybe you are creating the enemy by pushing yourself away and placing blame. Any enemy you encounter is not really an enemy. It is an extension of yourself, a learning experience. We can learn a lot from our enemies. They teach us to be true to our word, to be aware, and to never take advantage of a person or situation. Enemies are a blessing, without whom we would not appreciate our real friends. This does not mean that you need to go out and make your worst enemy your best friend. On the contrary, recognize the enemy for what he or she is: a learning experience. Instead of placing blame, ask, "What can be learned here?"

Learn from your enemies and unfortunate circumstances. In this way, you will never have to experience the lesson again.

Day 179
Responsibility

"Be the change you want to see in the world."

Mahatma Gandhi

Responsibility is the ability to respond. You are responsible for everything you say and do. Your response to any given situation is by your own choice. The feelings that occur within yourself, and the thoughts you think, are of your own doing. Placing blame, pointing the finger, and reacting negatively are all a result of uncontrolled emotions.

Be aware of the thoughts and emotions that arise within you at any given moment. Assume the responsibility for your chosen reaction.

Day 180
Consistency

"Part of courage is simple consistency."

Peggy Noonan

There is no substitute for being consistent. Take bowling, for instance. Anyone can bowl one strike, but it takes a lot of practice to bowl twelve strikes in a row for a perfect three hundred game. You need the right technique with the proper knowledge of the sport, just like for anything else in life. To be a musician, you must be able to play all the notes correctly in an entire song time after time, which comes only with practice and expertise. Most often people only become mediocre at anything, because they do too many things. If you want to excel at something, you need to dedicate time. You must have a natural love for whatever you are doing. In this way your chosen profession will be a labor of joy and enthusiasm.

Consistency is the key to success. You must focus your efforts and perfect your craft.

Day 181
Faith

"You block your dream when you allow your fear to grow bigger than your faith."

Mary Manin Morrissey

Belief in oneself is fundamentally the number one most important virtue of man. Lack of faith is the number one cause of all failures. We must believe to achieve. No matter what the obstacle, there is always a way to overcome such diversities. As we learn and grow, obstacles are created to test our faith—not only faith in ourselves, but also faith in the divine. It is for this reason that not all people have achieved their dreams in life. They either do not believe in themselves, or they don't believe in God. There has never been a story of success without problems. In fact, the greatest stories are the ones with the most adversity. Remember that your faith will make it so.

You are perfect, strong, and abundant. Everything you need comes quickly and easily.

Day 182
Pressure

"The only pressure I'm under is the pressure I've put on myself."

Mark Messier

What happens when you are faced with pressure? It comes in many different forms: deadlines at work, not having enough time in the day, family life, doing too much, having no money, having unpaid bills, etc. Do your daily tasks build and build to no end? Are you so stressed that you become physically sick? Are you angry or irritated most of the time? Maybe this is you, or maybe you know someone like this. Either way, this is pressure. The mind has taken over the body and is running your life on autopilot with maximum throttle engaged. Life was not meant to be lived like this. Things should be effortless and enjoyable. The fact is, there is always enough time; you just forgot how to enjoy the journey.

Begin by taking everything one step at a time. Whatever you are doing, give it your full attention. Refrain from thinking about what you need to do in a few hours from now, and focus on the task at hand.

Day 183
Wishes

"What a wonderful life I've had! I only wish I'd realized it sooner."

Sidonie Gabrielle

We all wish for things. We want our circumstances to be different, or we want to have more possessions. We always think we know better. However, how could we possibly know what we need more than the universe does? Why is it that we get frustrated when our wishes do not come true? Have you ever thought that there is a reason for not having something? Maybe you are not ready. You may think you are, but there must be something blocking it from happening. Also, the universe does not know the difference between our owning something and seeing it in reality. For instance, have you ever noticed that when you really want a specific car, soon in the future you see one on the road? Wishes are fantasy. They are great because we use our imagination, and if we are persistent enough, the wish will be fulfilled.

Be careful what you wish for; it just may come true. Thoughts become things. Always be mindful of your thoughts.

Day 184
Boasting

"Mules are always boasting that their ancestors were horses."

German Proverb

Boasting is selfish. There is no point in showing off or proving something to somebody else. It is only your ego trying to prove you are better because you can do something they cannot. However, when you are better at something, it is only because you have practiced it. In some rare cases, you will be better at something without ever having done it before. This makes you no better or worse than the other person. Under no circumstance should you ever boast about your achievements. There will always be someone better than you. However, it is always important to stay positive. Have fun and enjoy the fact that you are better. Play for fun and be pleased with your results. The fact that you win will not matter; it is simply about the sport.

Allow others to say how great you are. This is far better than anything you could ever say or show about yourself.

Day 185
Positivity

"Once you replace negative thoughts with positive ones, you'll start having positive results."

Willie Nelson

A positive mental attitude is vital to your well-being. The effects are great and profound. Negative self-talk leads to depression, anxiety, stress, and sickness. Positive self-talk promotes health, happiness, and prosperity. You will know if you are a positive person by the people who surround you on a daily basis. If people are generally kind toward you, smiling and laughing in your presence, and always greeting you openly, then you are a positive person. If people are mad around you, are always complaining and stressed, and are bitter and sarcastic, then you are a negative person. Remember, your outer world is a reflection of your inner being. Everything takes time. If you remain positive, your people and surroundings will change for the better.

To be positive in your mind is key to changing the world. When you are happy, the world around you is happy.

Day 186
Home

"Love begins by taking care of the closest ones—the ones at home."

Mother Teresa

Picture your home being your mind. Walk through your living quarters, look around, and picture it as if you were traveling deep inside your head, which in effect you are. If the outer world is truly a reflection of your inner being, then your home is the essence of your mind's eye. The place where you sleep and spend the most time is your world of thought manifested to reality. If your home has junk everywhere, is dirty and dusty, and disorganized, then you can be sure your mind is the same. If your home is clean, open, and well looked after, your mind is on the right track. Think about your home as if it were a computer. If your computer is properly maintained and defragmented, files will open quickly and easily and the computer will run smoothly. If it is not properly looked after, the computer will act sluggish and encounter many unforeseen issues.

Does your home need some cleaning? The less stuff you own, the less you have to worry about. Open space opens the mind.

Day 187
Choices

"You can lead a horse to water, but you can't make it drink."

Proverb

Life is filled with choices. Every day we must make hundreds of choices without even realizing it. We choose to go to work, smoke a cigarette, eat junk food, brush our teeth, get angry, curse, be honest, watch television, listen to radio, help someone, ask for assistance, etc. You may think that in some cases you do not have a choice, but you always do. Even if you don't notice it, a choice is always there. You are the creator of your own destiny. No one can make choices for you. When life has passed by and there is regret, it is you who is at fault. You are the one who refuses to let go. You are the one who chooses your mind-set. It is you who has to make the choice of peace.

With choice comes responsibility. You are responsible for all your actions and reactions. Placing blame injures your well-being.

Day 188
Regret

"Remorse is the poison of life."

Charlotte Bronte

There are times when you may feel you should have done something differently. Maybe it was something you said or did. Maybe it was something you didn't do. It could be the loss of a loved one and somehow you feel at fault. Whatever the reasoning, this is regret. No matter what happens from now on, it will not change the past. When regret occurs, you must let it go. Holding onto negative emotions takes away your energy and ability to function. For some it is easier to let go than it is for others. However, when attempting to let go of regret, you must face it. If you bury it, the feeling may lie dormant for a long period of time until something triggers its arrival again. If this happens, feel the pain and face it. You will soon find that the regret was really just something you thought was important to hold onto. It was a sense of self, created by the ego.

Let go and relax. Face the fear of regret. We all have something deep within. It is up to you to help yourself. There is nothing to fear.

DAY 189
GIVING UP

"Give up your selfishness, and you shall find peace; like water mingling with water, you shall merge in absorption."

Sri Guru Granth Sahib

At what point do you give up? When do you say enough is enough and change directions? There is a difference between giving up and giving in. Giving up means you have accepted failure. Giving in means you see the obstacles and work around them. You know there are thousands of ways to get where you want to go, so you must try another approach. To be submissive is not giving up. In fact, giving in is a natural part of the growth process. The more research and planning you do, the easier the path will be as you follow it. New ventures will always go in different directions. It is your choice to go down the path.

The next time you encounter an obstacle, look at it from an outsider's point of view. Think smart. The obstacle is there for a reason.

DAY 190
LATERAL THINKING

"All that we are is the result of what we have thought."

Buddha

Lateral thinking is a means by which one can solve problems through a creative approach. The term *lateral thinking* was coined by Edward de Bono in his 1967 book *New Think: The Use of Lateral Thinking.* In it, de Bono describes methods of thinking that are untraditional to typical human thought patterns. Often people perform the same tasks over and over again and get stuck in a rut. However, ideas are endless and abundant. There is no shortage of supply when it comes to creativity, yet most people think they will run out of this precious resource. Through creative problem solving, idea challenging, and other techniques, lateral thinking changes your thought patterns for a more creative, idea-enhancing result.

Traditional thought patterns can be thought of as vertical thinking. One will keep digging in the same spot, going deeper and deeper and finding no solution. In lateral thinking there are many solutions, which is like digging small holes in many different places.

Day 191
Reflective Listening

"Deep listening is miraculous for both listener and speaker. When someone receives us with openhearted, non-judging, intensely interested listening, our spirits expand."

Sue Patton Thoele

When people are speaking, 80 percent of what they are saying is transferred through body language. To be a good listener one must engage fully in the conversation. Most people do not listen at all. They are silent only in order to wait for the right moment to respond with their own verbiage. Reflective listening is the process by which you listen fully, not only to what a person is saying, but also to what they are feeling. In this way you can follow your heart for a response, as opposed to reacting with sarcasm or needlessly expressing a point of view. There is never a need to be right, only to be present. You may think reflective listening takes too much effort, which it will seem like at first. But as you become accustomed to listening intently with your entire body, you will find there are fewer arguments and negative feelings. As a result, your life and the lives of those around you will be happier and more fulfilled.

Listening is the key to communication. Most people fail to communicate properly simply because they do not know how to listen.

Day 192
Social Life

"In the End, we will remember not the words of our enemies, but the silence of our friends."

Martin Luther King Jr.

What kind of social life do you have? Do you find yourself surrounded by many friends most of the time? Do you have only one or two people you call your best friends? Are most people just acquaintances? As we grow older, our social life changes drastically. From adolescence to the late twenties, our social life thrives with new faces and experiences. Then something drastic happens. Our friends become married with children. Our need to go out dwindles as we are contented with being at home. People change their social habits as time moves on. Time becomes an enemy as every free moment seems fating and fleeting. Once there is a free moment, the last thing people want to do is go out and have a good time.

Are there people you would love to spend time with, yet neglect to call? What happened to having a good time with good people just for fun?

Day 193
Simplicity

"Small things amuse small minds."

Doris Lessing

Life is about enjoyment of the simple things. Desire nothing and find pleasure in the little tasks. Simplicity and all its beauty surround us. Nature: so simple yet so complex. Within complexity lies simplicity and vice versa. In today's society this saying has come to have a negative connotation. However, having a small mind implies little ego. Having little ego allows us to appreciate. Appreciating simple things is the enjoyment of being.

Take a moment today to enjoy something simple, a moment of appreciation for something beautiful.

Day 194
911

"And as ye would that men should do to you, do ye also to them likewise."

Luke 6:31

Many images come to mind when we think of this date in history. The most significant in recent history is that of the twin towers collapsing in 2001. How tragic and devastating the circumstances for many who were living and working in New York at the time. Within the blink of an eye, many firefighters and civilians came to the aid of the injured and dying. It is sad to think that someone planned to cause such immense devastation to humankind. It makes you think, how could there be people that have such little regard for others? This date in history is to be a reminder that no matter how far technologically we come, we must hold our neighbors in high regard. We are all living here together.

It is unfortunate that sometimes we must experience catastrophic events to appreciate what we have. Help others in any way you can. In effect, you are helping yourself.

Day 195
Teaching

"What nobler employment, or more valuable to the state, than that of the man who instructs the rising generation."

Marcus Tullius Cicero

To be a teacher is a great gift. Not everyone has the ability to teach. It must be developed and learned. To teach takes great communication skills. It takes not only this, but also patience, tolerance, and appreciation. Teaching is a two-way street. It takes full participation of the student and teacher. A great teacher realizes a lot can be learned from a student. As the lesson is taught, the teacher must be able to communicate the message in many different forms to accommodate the learning styles of the students. In this way, a teacher is always learning. Teaching is a skill that combines giving and receiving on an interpersonal level.

Do you teach others? What skills do you possess that can help others gain further knowledge? Do you have a teacher?

Day 196
Student

"Take the attitude of a student, never be too big to ask questions, never know too much to learn something new."

Og Mandino

To be a student takes discipline. One of the most common mistakes of the student is to get comfortable with the teacher and neglect to listen. Instead of using the teacher's wisdom, students think they know better. They sometimes think they know enough and so dismiss the lesson from the teacher. A great student knows the teacher has a wealth of knowledge and realizes that he or she is the student for a reason. A great student listens fully and intently and as a result, gains superior knowledge. Most times it is not the teacher who cannot relay the message, but the student who is not willing to listen. One must be humble to accept a lack of knowledge on a subject. It is not that the teacher is better than the student. It is that he or she has experience in a given field.

We are all students learning and growing. It is impossible to know everything. One must always listen and learn.

Day 197
Goal Check #4

"Some of the world's greatest feats were accomplished by people not smart enough to know they were impossible."

Doug Larson

After 196 days, how has your life changed? Has it changed at all? Are your surroundings different? Are your thoughts different? Do you desire the same things that you did before? Write down your desires again. Are they limited to yourself, or are they more humanitarian? Either way, this is fine. Be true to your heart's desire. Deep inside of you is a purpose that is to be fulfilled. Nobody but you knows what this purpose is. By assessing your goals, you will come closer and closer to who you were meant to be.

Take five minutes and do this now, or at some point today. It will help you more than you know.

Day 198
Comparing

"In life there is always going to be someone better than you."

Jerry Flanagan

Many people often feel the need to compare themselves with others. We need to know if we are smarter, stronger, faster, better at something, etc. This comparison leads to competition and separation. Anyone can be good or fast or whatever he or she wants at anything. All anything takes is practice and patience. There will always also be someone who is worse. But what is the difference? Who cares? You care. Why do you care? Only you know the answer. Know that when you stop caring, the need for competition fades. The only competition you ever have is with yourself.

We are all unique and different. We all have our talents and downfalls. Comparing is not the answer. Improving yourself is.

Day 199
Boss

"No man goes before his time, unless the boss leaves early."

Groucho Marx

Most companies have bosses. Such a situation creates resentment. Productivity and creativity suffer when we have to answer to someone. The best companies in the world are those that are based on teamwork. There is no hierarchy where workers get told what to do. Picture a family. Everyone has a specific role: mother, father, son, or daughter. When a person is aware of his or her role, the family is in harmony, listening to one another. There is no boss. However, if a son or daughter misbehaves, one of the parents will intervene. This is like a job with no boss. Everyone has a role, but they do not push around their statuses. If one person does not act according to protocol, that person will be spoken to. However, it is not a case of being higher or better. Every role is needed for the family—or the organization—to survive and thrive.

What type of working environment are you involved in? Do you enjoy your work? What roles are you playing throughout the day?

Day 200
Gossip

"I don't at all like knowing what people say of me behind my back. It makes me far too conceited."

Oscar Wilde

When upset with the way someone acts, you may have the inclination to talk about it. Some people are never able to let something go. They will continue to talk badly about a person for hours, days, or weeks on end. Doing this brings the energy of that person or situation to the conversation. When you speak badly about someone, the only person it hurts is you. That negative energy clings to you and will be there until it is let go. There is no reason to gossip. All it does is feed the ego's need to be right, making the other person wrong. Gossip is one of the primary dysfunctions of human behavior. Its only purpose is to separate us from one another.

The next time you catch yourself speaking badly about someone, know that it is you who is suffering.

Day 201
Bowling

"Just play. Have fun. Enjoy the game."

Michael Jordan

Bowling is an amazing sport. Anyone can pick up a bowling ball, throw it down the lane, and get one strike. But to be consistent and knock all the pins down most of the time takes practice, technique, and the right frame of mind. It takes many years to be a professional bowler. It is amazing how something so simple can be enjoyed by so many. Every time you bowl, it is the exact same situation. All that needs to be done is to hit all the pins down. Yet different circumstances lead to different frames of mind. Various lane conditions lead to varying results. The possibilities are endless, yet the idea is always the same. Go up there and knock them all down.

It is the simple things in life that are enjoyable. Bowling is fun and competitive. It's for people of all ages. Go bowling!

Day 202
Judgments

"Judge not, and ye shall not be judged."

Luke 6:37

You will never truly know someone, no matter how much time you spend with him or her. They say you must walk a mile in another person's shoes. Even if you walked for ten years in a person's shoes, you would still never know him or her fully. Everyone is different and everyone is connected. To judge the actions of others is not right. Who they are is not what they have done. We are not what we think, do, or say. Therefore, one can never determine the true nature of a person through actions or hearsay. If you think people have done wrong, take note of it. Make it a point to learn from their experiences and to never do it yourself. You cannot change others. You can only change yourself. So change yourself and watch in amazement as the world changes around you.

Take responsibility for your thoughts and actions. Any fault you see in others is a fault of your own.

Day 203
First Impressions

"The key to good decision making is not knowledge. It is understanding."

Malcolm Gladwell

It has been proved that our feelings within the first two seconds of an interaction will give us all the information we need about a person or situation. Students were asked to watch five-second video clips of teachers and determine whether they were good or bad at their professions. They were also asked what kind of personality the teachers had and whether they liked their demeanors. With stunning 90 percent accuracy, the students watching the five-second clips gave the same information about the teachers as the students who had been in their classes for an entire semester. This is truly fascinating. Something about us knows instantly about what a person is like within the first couple of seconds before the mind takes over and judges the interaction.

Take notice of your first reaction to people and situations. Learn to listen to your body and trust your instincts.

Day 204
For the Birds

"God loved the birds and invented trees. Man loved the birds and invented cages."

Jacques Deval

For Christmas one year a son bought his father a beautiful bird feeder. The father did not like any of the old feeders because he couldn't tell when the food was finished. Also, the squirrels would get into them. This new feeder had a completely clear body and a ledge for the birds to sit on as they ate. If an animal was too heavy, the ledge would slide down and close the doors to the food. The gift was perfect. When the feeder was installed, the birds would come and eat the food. However, the birds would now fly over, throw down the food, and allow the squirrels to eat from the ground.

Nature has a way of showing us things we would have never realized. There is abundance for everyone. The birds and the squirrels have more than enough food to go around.

Day 205
Perseverance

"There is no substitute for hard work."

Thomas Edison

To accomplish anything great takes perseverance. Through diligence of practice, hard work, and dedication, one can achieve great feats. The trouble is, most people stop after experiencing their first hurdle. We must realize that no matter what the chosen field, there will be obstacles. The situations vary depending on our ways of thinking and beliefs. We can do anything and become anything. The world is here for us, and its primary function is to make us happy. Through perseverance of mind, body, and faith we can accomplish greatness. We say "mind" because you must think as if you have already attained your hopes and dreams. In your mind, there is no other alternative. Be happy and appreciative of what you have. With your body you must perform the actions to attain your dream. And finally, through faith, you must open up to the possibility of the impossible. You must believe it will happen with your entire being.

Believe you can achieve, and it will happen. Any great accomplishment comes with defeats and setbacks.

Day 206
Chances

"No guts, no glory."

Garfield

You must take chances to succeed. Most people want to change their lives, but never change what they are doing. They keep working the same job that makes them unhappy, living in the same house, doing the same things. Yet they want change. Change does not happen without chance. Chances do not occur without change. You must change your ways of thinking and doing.

Chance and change go hand in hand. Let go of the fear of loss. You may be too comfortable.

Day 207
Excitement

"Get excited and enthusiastic about your own dream. This excitement is like a forest fire—you can smell it, taste it, and see it from a mile away."

Denis Waitley

The greatest way to bring about positive change in your life is to be excited about something. When we are excited there is joy in our being, with a sense of innocence and childlikeness. Excitement is positive and is the highest level of enthusiasm. When we are bored, sad, negative, angry, worried, etc., it is impossible to be excited. Negative emotions change our thinking into the opposite of excitement and do more harm than good. It is impossible to be negative when we're excited. Think about joyous outcomes and circumstances. Get caught up in the now moment and let the time fly by.

What makes you excited? What drives you to practice and succeed? What delivers to you the true joy of being? It is different for everyone.

Day 208
Vacations

"I travel not to go anywhere, but to go. I travel for travel's sake. The great affair is to move."

Robert Louis Stevenson

Everyone needs to get away. For many different reasons, most people never travel. They make up excuse after excuse, like there is not enough time or not enough money. They continually say they can't do this or that. However, traveling and exploring are natural parts of life. Everyone must travel and grow. Always be sure to put money aside in a travel fund to go on vacation at least once a year. We are evolving beings who need space and new surroundings. Much can be learned from travel and experiences. Some people travel, but they always go to the same place. This is not exploration. This is comfort. A true healthy way of travel is to explore new destinations. Obtain new knowledge of a culture by living its global reality for a period of time.

Traveling elevates your presence and state of mind by opening you up to new and exciting possibilities.

Day 209
Failure

"Failure is not an option."

Apollo 13

Failing at something is a natural part of the growing process. There is not a single successful person who did not fail at times during the process of getting to where he or she is. The problem is that most people never even try, because they are afraid of failure. The truth is, you are bound to fail at something. A great example is lifting weights at the gym. In order to build muscle, we must train to failure, meaning we must lift until the body cannot push the weight anymore. It is the last two lifts that build the muscle. Failures make us grow and evolve. They guide us to our true calling. If you haven't failed at something, you're not on the right path. It is like tryouts. Those who really love it and want to be it try and try again.

Think of an obstacle that you had to overcome. Notice how it made you stronger and provided virtue.

Day 210
Money

"It's not about the money."

Bob Proctor

In our societal existence money seems to be one of the most important factors to our survival. Note that even though we think we need money, it's not really the case. Money is important only because of what it allows us to purchase. With money one can attain a home, buy food, drive a car, buy clothes, and do pretty much anything. Someone's lack of money is not some external factor. It is something within the individual. In many cultures around the world they do not have money. They not only survive, they thrive through the joy and happiness of being. Many think that money will bring them happiness. The only true happiness is in this now moment. Future events will never bring joy and fulfillment unless you are happy now. A lack of money is never the issue. We are connected to infinite source and abundance. The problem is we have forgotten who we are.

What is it that money can buy for you that motivates you to succeed? What is it that money can't buy that drives you to become a better person?

Day 211
Natural Talent

"Put yourself on view. This brings your talents to light."

Baltasar Gracian

Have you ever noticed that some people are born with talent? It seems as though they effortlessly excel at some form of sport, art, activity, or vocation. Sometimes, even at a young age, an unexplainable amount of pure talent originates from a person. Where does this knowledge come from? It is said we all have a destiny, a life blueprint. We all have something deep within us, our true passion. When we find our true calling, work is effortless. In fact, there is no such thing as work, because it is our heart's desire. Your natural abilities coincide with the desire to learn and grow. With ease and happiness your true vocation is realized and achieved.

What is your true calling? Do you have any natural talents? What do you love to do now that you would do for free?

Day 212
Difficulties

"I can be changed by what happens to me, but I refuse to be reduced by it."

Maya Angelou

There is no such thing as a difficult situation. The only difficulty is in your mind. We make things out to be not as they are. The world knows no difficulty or lack. Everything simply is. When difficulties arise in whatever form, know that there is always a way. In fact, hardships are given to us for a reason. Everyone must go through obstacles and challenges to learn the lessons of life. A difficulty is an illusion, just like everything else we experience. A negative attitude elicited by an obstacle is the difficulty. A positive frame of mind is needed at all times. Clear your thoughts and move forward effortlessly.

The world is yours for the enjoyment of being. Your only difficulty is a negative mind.

DAY 213
RUMORS

"Never make negative comments or spread rumors about anyone. It depreciates their reputation and yours."

Brian Koslow

Why must people take part in negative speak about other people? He said this, or she did that. There is no place for this. The only thing a rumor does is inflate the ego. It separates people into thinking they are right and the other person is wrong. Then groups of people join one side or the other. Political parties use rumors to have large numbers of people pick one side or the other. This is not how friends should act, nor should it dictate how a country is operated. Rumors do nothing but spread negativity. To cultivate peace and compassion, one must never participate in rumors or anything of the sort. When people say or do something you dislike, make a mental note of it. Remember, the outer world is a reflection of your inner being.

Rumors and names are used by the weak. You are strong and beautiful. One with all that is. Just like the people who start the rumors.

Day 214
Holidays

"A vacation is what you take when you can no longer take what you've been taking."

Earl Wilson

Sometimes we just need some space from the everyday, some time to be at home or at the cottage. Just to unwind and think. It is important to clear your head and relax. This is no reason to binge on drugs or alcohol. This is a great time to let go and be free. Take a day trip to somewhere you wouldn't normally go. Talk to people whom you haven't seen in a while. Have some fun and take it easy. We are here to enjoy ourselves.

How do you see yourself spending a holiday? You do not need to go anywhere. Just get away from the monotony of the everyday.

Day 215
Maturity

"The rate at which a person can mature is directly proportional to the embarrassment he can tolerate."

Douglas Engelbart

As we grow older, there is a certain level of maturity that needs to be maintained. This is a general knowledge of appropriate behavior in various circumstances. Maintaining a level of maturity is a must to be accepted amongst social groups and to gain the respect of peers. However, most people take maturity too seriously. It is thought that being mature means not having fun. A person with this frame of mind remains serious at all times. This could not be further from the truth. Being mature means knowing where to draw the line in terms of speech, action, and responsibility. One can be open and exhibit childlike behavior, yet still be mature. In fact, we should always exercise the child within ourselves. This is the key to happiness.

Being mature is mandatory in our society. Often it is misconstrued as being serious. Look at the world through a child's eyes with honesty, sincerity, and a sense of humor.

Day 216
Weather

"There is no such thing as bad weather, only different kinds of good weather."

John Ruskin

We are one with all that is. This includes the weather. Have you ever noticed that when it is cloudy and rainy you may have a headache or feel fatigued? Or when it is sunny and hot you have more energy? This is because we are the weather. Our collective unconscious creates what we experience together as a whole. This is why some cultures perform rain dances in order to change the weather. If we believe wholeheartedly that we can change the weather, it will change. Why does this work? Do you believe that you are connected to everything? If so, then what makes the weather any different?

We influence, and are influenced by, everything around us. The weather plays a part in our thoughts and feelings. Notice how different aspects of weather affect your mood.

Day 217
Artwork

"The hospitals save our souls; the arts feed them."

Michael Grit

Collecting works of art is a joy and a privilege. No matter how many painters, sculptors, sketch artists, or photographers there are, no two works will ever be the same. We all have different talents. Our individualism shines through art. Collecting art brings about an appreciation for the creativity and talents of others. They are conversation pieces. What is also interesting is the difference in art from other parts of the world. Not only the style, but also the mediums differ. It is inspiring to see the amount of detail and love that goes into a single work. It is all subjective, and monetary values are in the eye of the beholder.

Do you have an appreciation for the arts? What is your favorite type of work? Do you have any around the house?

Day 218
Reading

"The more that you read, the more things you will know. The more that you learn, the more places you'll go."

Dr. Seuss

Reading is one of our fundamental, most important ways to learn and grow. It allows the individual the ability to move across the paper and discover information at his or her own pace. Watching television or listening to audio does not provide the same balanced learning as reading. It takes focus, discipline, and desire to successfully read a book. This book is broken down day by day for a reason. One could probably read all the pages in a single day, but he or she would be missing the point. The words here are designed to be absorbed and pondered. We all learn at different rates and read at different levels. Reading is truly a blessing and should be exercised on a daily basis. Reading the right materials enhances our speech, creativity, and knowledge.

One can always tell if someone reads by the way he or she speaks. Those who convey messages with ease are the knowledgeable and gifted.

Day 219
Speaking

"Speaking comes by nature, silence by understanding."

German Proverb

Speech is the most commonly used form of communication known to man. The words we choose and our manner of delivery influence how a person thinks and feels. Our vocabulary is vital to our existence on this planet. You may never have thought language to be so important. If you are in disbelief, try moving to a foreign country for a couple of months where they do not speak your native language. You will see how vital oral communication really is. Imagine everyone in the world spoke a different language. There would be chaos and segregation. English is amongst the most commonly used languages in the world, and so unites billions of people. It is very important to always be sincere and truthful. Use language as a tool, not a weapon. Our ability to speak is a gift that should not be taken for granted.

In a world where speech is vital to our survival, there is no place for sarcasm or negativity. Always be sincere and truthful.

Day 220
Romance

"A true man does not need to romance a different girl every night, a true man romances the same girl for the rest of her life."

Ana Alas

Affection from someone close is beneficial on so many levels. Being romantic and spontaneous with your partner is wonderful. It takes true passion to be completely and honestly romantic with someone. If love is not felt deep down inside, the romantic level of a relationship can only be physical. Physical passion lasts only so long. Eventually the fire that was once felt for a person fades with time. It is easy to fall into a serious relationship quickly, thinking it is the right choice. However, as time marches on, the relationship could do more harm than good. Romance is not only physical and sexual, but also mental. It takes thought, dedication, and selflessness. A true romantic endeavor is accomplished out of free will and appreciation. One takes the time to know a person intimately, and therefore is able to give without the need for compensation … although the giver is fully compensated by the joy and happiness in his or her partner.

What are your partner's likes and dislikes? How can you please him or her today with a small gesture of your appreciation?

Day 221
Significant Other

"A divorce is like an amputation: you survive it, but there's less of you."

Margaret Atwood

To think there is only one right person for you is absurd. As we change and evolve, the person who was once right may grow into someone completely different. A genuine life partner is someone you can grow and learn with. It is impossible to be the same all your life. Every cell in our bodies replenishes itself within a few years. That is to say, if our physical bodies evolve at such a rapid pace, how is it that our personalities do not? You really have someone special if he or she understands and cares for your basic needs. This is, however, a two-way street. A relationship has its ups and downs, and if you truly love someone with all your heart, you will be open and honest on all subjects. It is you who chooses your life partner, so choose wisely.

It is said that each of is one-half of a soul. Everyone has a life partner. Whether you meet in this life or the next is a different story.

Day 222
Ownership

"Love does not cause suffering: what causes it is the sense of ownership, which is love's opposite."

Antoine de Saint-Exupery

What does it mean to own something? Did you know that our subconscious mind does not know the difference between ownership and seeing? For instance, when we see a beautiful sports car being driven down the highway, our subconscious has attracted that car to us. Regardless of whether you own it or not, you've attracted it. Ownership is something created by the ego. To think that something is "mine" indicates that you are thinking you are a separate entity from all that is. Worldly possessions are fleeting and will never be who you are. In our lifetime we acquire many things. Regardless of whether you pay for something, or it is given to you, if people believe it's yours, then you possess it. If you want something, you first must believe you have it; the world will follow. True happiness has no owner.

You are divine spirit in human form. You can manifest anything. Believe to achieve. You are not your possessions.

Day 223
Costumes

"I see my face in the mirror and go, 'I'm a Halloween costume? That's what they think of me?'"

Drew Carey

It is always great to step out of character for a day and act like someone, or something else. Costumes allow us to put on a show for the people around us. There is something adventurous about dressing up. Actors do this all the time. To be a believable character takes a great deal of discipline and talent. Great actors are able to make their roles so believable that the audience feels a connection with them. Oftentimes, people think they know someone because they saw him or her in a movie. How could this be true? The actor was playing a role. However it came to be, the actor has touched the person's heart by relating to something within him or her. This is the beautiful part about dressing up and acting. One can relate to someone on a completely different level than just listening and being sympathetic.

We watch actors on a daily basis on television and in movies. Our life seems to revolve around acting. Why not embrace this game of role-playing even for a day?

Day 224
Support

"A friend is the one who comes in when the whole world has gone out."

Grace Pulpit

It is very important to have the support of those close to you. Whether it's from family, friends, or a significant other, support is needed to succeed. The greatest men and women of our time all had the love and support of those closest to them. Little is written about the warm-heartedness and unconditional love of a spouse or family member contributing to society. However, it is very necessary indeed. With the ups and downs of life, we need the reassurance of a trusting source that we are on the right path. Often, when we are concerned with the greater good, the road can seem long and arduous. Yet there is always hope. It is those we love most who are the real source of life. Their support and good intentions are all we need to be great.

Cultivate the appreciation for those around you. Those who love you most are your main source of inspiration. You are those you love.

Day 225
Destiny

"Destiny is no matter of chance. It is a matter of choice: it is not a thing to be waited for, it is a thing to be achieved."

William Jennings Bryan

We all have a destiny, a purpose. We are destined to do great things. We have a burning desire to attain and grow. Destiny is our guided path. Whether we choose to accept this or not is a different story. Life is easier when you feel you are meant to do something. As a matter of fact, we are destined to do exactly what we are doing right now. You were destined to read this, which may or may not put you on a path to succeed. Your destiny is yours and yours alone. No one can tell you what you are meant to do. Only you know deep down inside what it is that makes you happy. What makes you happy is your destiny. If staying at home with your children makes you happy, then fulfill your destiny. Your destiny is always something positive, and thus contributes to the greater good of humanity. Your destiny is never something negative. If you think it is, you are on the wrong path. Killing, stealing, pillaging, and other forms of abuse are never a true calling.

You are meant for something great. You have a purpose to be fulfilled. You will know you have completed your destiny when your time as a human is over.

Day 226
Pets

"The purity of a person's heart can be quickly measured by how they regard animals."

Immanuel Kant

Most people have a pet at some point in their lives, whether it's a cat, dog, bird, hamster, fish, or turtle. What is it about having an animal to call our own? It is that loving warmth. A connection with an animal is different than that with a human. When people care for an animal, they are doing so out of the goodness of their hearts. However, there are a lot of people who neglect animals. A huge responsibility comes with owning a pet. A lot of people pay attention to the animal a great deal within the first couple of weeks. Then when the novelty wears off, they forget the animal exists. Some people abuse their cats or dogs by hitting them and yelling at them. This is not right. An animal is a pet to be loved. The bond between a human and an animal can be very strong and beautiful if one shows patience, tolerance, and compassion.

Think back to when you had a pet, or even right now. Is your pet happy? Do you give it the love and care it needs?

Day 227
School

"If you think education is expensive, try ignorance."

Andy McIntyre

There are things you would never know if you didn't go to school. You could be in a vocation all your life and be missing that one bit of information that would be the last piece of the puzzle. It takes humbleness to go back to school after having worked for many years. There is always something more to learn. No matter what industry you are in, schooling always helps. Many think they do not need school because they don't teach you real knowledge. This is why it is important to attend a school with industry professionals with real-life experience. Schooling may seem like a step in the wrong direction, but it's not. To attend school may delay your plans for achieving goals, but in the long run it's worth the wait. What is an extra year or two in the grand scheme of your life?

Do you need more education to be where you want to be? Never be afraid to learn. It is never too late to start over.

Day 228
Goal Check #5

"Only those who will risk going too far can possibly find out how far one can go."

T. S. Eliot

What kinds of obstacles have you been experiencing in reaching the goals you set out to accomplish? Are these obstacles stopping you from moving forward? Are they becoming excuses for you to not continue on your chosen path? Do you need to change directions to continue forward? Every day you can do something to attain your goal. It is all about the little things that add up. You cannot build a skyscraper overnight. Big goals can seem daunting at first. Take the small steps every day to achieve success. What can you do right now to progress forward in the right direction?

Life is an accumulation of little efforts that paint a bigger picture. Focus on the now and have a plan.

Day 229
Advertising

"Advertising is the art of convincing people to spend money they don't have for something they don't need."

Will Rogers

Our minds absorb thousands of advertisements every day. Without realizing it, we are influenced by surroundings with simple visual cues. We recognize brands, and have knowledge of a product or service, even if we have no interest in what they offer. The power of advertising is outrageous! Advertisers play on our needs and desires to make us think a certain way. Billions of dollars are put into advertising every year, and it's no wonder. Advertising works, if done correctly. One can sell anything if it's marketed to the right demographic in the proper manner. To be a successful business owner, one must cultivate the use of advertising and marketing. With the right mind-set, one can be aware when he or she is taken advantage of. In this way one will not easily succumb to manipulation.

Know that you are advertising yourself every day. You are your own marketing team. How you dress and act influences others and determines your success.

Day 230
Remembering

"Lest we forget."

Rudyard Kipling

It is important to be reminded of times of tribulation and turmoil. The world of man has gone through many wars and much bloodshed. There will be a time when we no longer kill one another, but that day seems to stretch further and further away. It is important to recall our mistakes. Remember the people who fought for freedom. Humanity is its own worst enemy. We shall never forget these times of war and refuge as a new age dawns. This new age will bring an era of peace and harmony. We must stand firm in our convictions and peaceful authority. There is no room in this world for murder and torment. We are spiritual beings who thrive on love. There is no love in war, only sorrow and misery.

Remember always that we are ignorant. We wage war on each other with little regard for human life. Be grateful for our freedom.

Day 231
Changes

"The doors we open and close each day decide the lives we live."

Flora Whittemore

The process we must undergo to change our lives is sometimes daunting and bleak. One can feel the void when there is something missing. This feeling of discontent transforms into a burning desire to succeed. So many choices. So many options. Where does one begin? What does your heart tell you? You can be anything, and do anything. Change is necessary, yet the path is not always clear. One seeks the guidance of loved ones only to be more confused. Everyone has a different opinion. No one really knows what is ultimately right for you. Lead with your heart, and the rest will follow.

The time of change is upon us. Are you ready to make the leap forward? If you were not seeking change, you would not be reading this.

Day 232
Leading with Heart

"The heart has reasons that reason does not understand."

Jacques Benigne Bossuel

How do you know if your heart is in the right place? How do you know your chosen path is correct? To obtain an answer, you must answer the following question truthfully: Am I helping someone? If the answer is no, then this is good. Leading with the heart is most often a gut instinct. There is this impulse to do something. Deep down inside we all have the capacity to love and be loved. This is the fundamental basic human function. When we lead with our hearts, our true desires and abilities are exercised to their fullest potential. We are divine spirits who purposefully explore new realms of learning. Your deepest desires will always be your own and can only be unlocked through self-exploration.

Follow your dreams. The course will lead you on unimaginable roads to your destined outcome and beyond.

Day 233
Networking

"It's not what you know, but who you know."

Robert Kerrigan

Networking is the most important aspect of any career. Pretend for a moment you are a musician. You are a very good performer with impeccable songwriting. When listening to the radio you get frustrated because the music being played is dull and boring. You think to yourself, *Why isn't it my music being played?* There is one simple explanation. You have not talked to the right people. There are necessary steps in every industry, and the doors of opportunity open to those who poke their heads through. It's easy to get lost in the shuffle with so many talented people all around. One must stand out and be proud of his or her accomplishments. Meeting the right people will help you in more ways than you can imagine.

Every person has a circle of friends. Every person within that circle of friends has a different circle that they are also a part of. Ten people in a room together know one thousand people very closely.

Day 234
Loss

"Death is not the greatest loss in life. The greatest loss is what dies inside us while we live."

Norman Cousins

The world always balances itself out. With every loss there is gain. We may not see the gain at first, because we are so close to the loss that it's like not being able to see the forest through the trees. As told by Napoleon Hill, every loss carries the seed of an equal or greater benefit. We must focus on the positive to attain goals. When adversity strikes, be steadfast and upright. Know that you are on the right path. This is a world of opposites. The loss of a loved one, a job, a friend, or anything else contains something great. We just need to look closely to find what that something is. Great is the time of loss as we grow to new heights.

Stay positive; your time will come. Your loss is one of many, just like your gains.

Day 235
Waiting

"Waiting is a trap. There will always be reasons to wait. The truth is, there are only two things in life, reasons and results, and reasons simply don't count."

Dr. Robert Anthony

Sometimes it is difficult to remain patient. When financial difficulties arise, stress, anxiety, and worry may dominate your thoughts. Never forget your true nature and abilities. Remember, the bigger the goal, the longer and harder the road. But it does not have to be so. Something is hard only if you make it out to be. Waiting is a time of self-renewal. It is a natural part of the growing process. We all want to see our lives be successful and happy without any bumps in the road. One cannot succeed without times of waiting. It is a true test of beliefs and foresight. To wait is to gain strength. Gather your strength and energy for the long road ahead.

It is only waiting if you choose it to be so. In a doctor's office you sit in a waiting room. The time can pass fast or slow depending on your frame of mind.

Day 236
Independence

"True independence and freedom can only exist in doing what's right."

Brigham Young

What does it mean to be independent? Is it financial freedom? Living on your own? Having a family? Whatever the case, independence means responsibility. It is the knowledge that you are accountable for everything you say and do. You must be true to your word and respect the wishes of others. Some people think independence means not relying on others. This could not be further from the truth. One needs the help of others to be independent. Work with people, provide a product or service, and be a team player. One gains independence through interactions with others. You must earn your independence by relying on yourself to aid others. It is not just a right; it is a privilege.

Your independence is not based solely on your ability to live alone. It is based on the ability to work cooperatively with others.

Day 237
Smoking

"I love to smoke. I smoke a thousand packs a day and I'm never quitting."

Denis Leary

Why do people smoke? Many have different excuses. The addiction will make up all kinds of reasons to harm your body. It's understandable that people cannot quit smoking, but why start in the first place? To quit smoking after many years is a great accomplishment. Many fail to quit, because they are not in the right frame of mind. You must be fully ready and able to take it one day at a time. There is no reason to start smoking. It is simply negligent to your body and those around you. In the news the other day, there was an overweight two-year-old who smokes two packs a day. We immediately point our finger at the parent. However, on a deeper level we are all responsible for that child smoking. How can we be so naive? We are to blame for the unfortunate circumstances of the world. When will we learn to stop harming ourselves?

Not smoking is very basic. Smoking should not even be considered by any human being. Why harm yourself? You deserve better.

Day 238
Five Minutes

"We'll take a five-minute break while I go give myself hell."

Antal Dorati

Your life can completely change in five minutes. A day can be broken up into little segments and habits. For instance, it takes five minutes to smoke a cigarette. In five minutes you can also take a shower, brush your teeth, write a paragraph, draw a picture, meditate, or read a couple of pages in a book. When we view our lives in this way, it is a lot easier to change bad habits. Also, creating new habits is a lot easier if approached in this fashion. It is easy to do something for five minutes. It is also easy to not do something and replace that five minutes with something else. Picture a smoker who goes through a pack a day. That is roughly twenty cigarettes multiplied by five minutes. That means this person spends one hundred minutes in a day smoking. Imagine you took that one hundred minutes and did something more productive.

Make a list of all the five minutes you spend in a single day. Are there times you would like to cut out? Is there something you would rather be doing?

Day 239
Skills

"A person might be an expert in any field of knowledge or a master of many material skills and accomplishments. But without inner cleanliness his brain is a desert waste."

Sri Sathya Sai Baba

There are so many skills and trades it is impossible to be good at them all. The possibilities are endless, and to be a professional takes time, focus, and dedication. One of the most common mistakes a person can make is being mediocre at a lot of things instead of being truly spectacular at one skill. The people who are successful are those who choose one talent and work toward it. Michael Jordan is not a great hockey player. Eddie Vedder is not an excellent accountant. Eddie Murphy is not a great bowler. These are examples of successful people who have chosen a profession and made it their lives. Only when you focus your skills and talents will success come to you. Stay positive, be sincere with yourself, and choose your heart's desire. Your destiny is in your own hands.

Your skills and developments through life guide you on your chosen path. Utilize your skills to attain a focused, successful career.

DAY 240
ASK

"For everyone that asketh, receiveth: and he that seeketh, findeth: and to him that knocketh, it shall be opened."

Matthew 7:8

Often people wonder why they do not receive a desired outcome. The answer is simple. You have forgotten to ask. Not many people can read minds. This is truer than you realize. Sometimes what we ask for takes a while, but it always comes. Some people will work and work, while others just sit and watch. The person who works eventually gets upset because no one is helping. However, the person never asked. There is no harm in asking. It does not make you weak or any less of a person. It takes a truly confident person to know when he or she needs help.

If you know you need assistance, ask. Your friends and family will always be willing to help if you are in need. It makes them feel important.

Day 241
Anticipation

"An intense anticipation itself transforms possibility into reality, our desires being often but precursors of the things which we are capable of performing."

Samuel Smiles

Do you remember when you were a child and it was the night before Christmas? It was seemingly impossible to sleep, because you would know that when morning came, Santa Claus would have delivered presents. The magical imagination of a child is so powerful that anything is possible. It is that excitement with anticipation that provides joy and happiness. The next morning you wake up and run down the stairs. Presents are under the tree, and it's finally time to open gifts. The joy of being an innocent child in anticipation is a wonder. The greatest gift ever given to us was innocence. As we grow older, our curiosity lessens and moments of joyous anticipation seem few and far between.

Joy and excitement from anticipation come from being happy with who you are. A child awaiting Santa Claus is a person in a magical world where anything is possible. Beautiful, isn't it?

Phase IV—Knowledge

Conscious Levels, Numbers, Chakras, Senses, Colors, and Education

Day 242
Knowledge

"There is one thing one has to have: either a soul that is cheerful by nature, or a soul made cheerful by work, love, art, and knowledge."

Friedrich Nietzsche

The ability to remember, gain insight, and learn is beyond comprehension. We are gifted and talented. To retain information and use it in daily practice is an unfathomable gift from God. Interestingly, no matter how much knowledge we acquire, we always search for more. The thirst for knowledge is a gift almost as great as knowledge itself. Reading, writing, drawing, learning, painting, making music, and playing games are all great pastimes. They are called pastimes because that is what they do. They pass the time. Have you noticed that when you really enjoy something, the time seems to disappear at a rapid pace? Let your enjoyment flow through all pores of your body. Be one with the present moment.

Use your spare time to gain knowledge in whatever area of life you wish. Have fun with it.

Day 243
Consciousness Levels

"If you view all the things that happen to you, both good and bad, as opportunities, then you operate out of a higher level of consciousness."

Les Brown

Every day, people go through high levels of consciousness and low levels depending on their thoughts and feelings. Most people are stuck at low levels, and because of their association with form, they see glimpses of higher levels only for brief moments. The main goal is to awaken and allow consciousness to flow through you. This means to be completely at peace with any external circumstance. To put it simply, the more peaceful you are, the more consciousness flows through you. Consciousness never changes; only our thoughts and feelings change, which allow more or less consciousness to flow through us. The higher we vibrate, the higher levels we achieve. For the next nine days we will be looking at our emotions and discussing the effects they have on our consciousness level. The human body was designed for the purpose of manifesting consciousness into this world. You will learn how your state of mind plays a significant role in the totality of human existence.

As the days progress, monitor your thoughts as best you can. Don't try to change them; just notice them.

Day 244
Shame

"A man should never be ashamed to own that he has been in the wrong, which is but saying ... that he is wiser today than yesterday."

Jonathan Swift

This is the lowest level of consciousness. It is also known as apathy. When one is in this place, there is depression, boredom, and negativity. People have been known to commit suicide when submersed in these feelings for too long. This is a negative, never-ending, downward spiral. Your mind is like a runaway train, always finding something wrong with a situation and consistently saying you are worthless. This could not be further from the truth; however, when you are in this state of mind it is difficult to break free. The ego has taken over and is feeding off your neediness. When all your energy is drained, the ego will seek energy from other sources, like your loved ones. It will lash out and accuse. Shame is by far the lowest level of consciousness, yet so many people experience this daily.

If you experience any of these emotions, stop! Take some deep breaths and calm your mind. Find inner space and relax. Be present now.

Day 245
Grief

"He that conceals his grief finds no remedy for it."

Turkish Proverb

As the consciousness level rises, it does so exponentially. This means that to achieve a higher level is not as simple as going from one step to the other. However, because shame and grief are negative levels of consciousness, they are easy to achieve. It is when we get to the positive levels that there are significant boundaries of exploration which are not normally seen in Western society. Grief is the feeling of unhappiness. It generally means that we take all misfortunes personally. When we are in this situation, we feel unloved, sad, betrayed, ignored, or guilty. We often experience grief when a loved one dies. Sometimes this feeling can last for weeks, months, or even years. This is a very serious situation if it exists for long periods of time, as it will ultimately lead to depression and therefore cause shame.

Grieving a loss is natural; however, it must be let go. There is no point in holding onto grief or any other negative emotion.

Day 246
Fear

"The key to change is to let go of fear."

Rosanne Cash

Fear is the most common emotion in our collective society to this date. We are constantly bombarded with news and advertisements eliciting the fear of not fitting in, war, poverty, scarcity, etc. Marketing and news corporations know the power of fear, and so use it to manipulate the masses into thinking and acting in certain ways. Fear prevents us from having and doing the things we love. Most people stay with a job they do not like for the fear of not having security. Most people live uneventful lives for the purpose of creating a life they cannot afford. Feelings associated with fear include worry, nervousness, shyness, or a sense of being threatened, trapped, or defensive.

Every human being has some sort of fear, whether it is on the surface or deep-seated. Facing your fears is the first step toward freeing yourself and becoming who you were meant to be.

Day 247
Lust

"Whether we fall by ambition, blood, or lust, like diamonds we are cut with our own dust."

John Webster

Lust is a feeling of want that advertising takes advantage of in today's society. By giving a false sense of identity, products and needless desires are pushed to the masses on a daily basis. Some of the emotions associated with lust are selfishness, greed, envy, impatience, and overindulgence. Lust is a negative emotion, yet it is higher than fear. Lust can lead to greater things, such as achieving goals. However, when you are driven by lust, no amount of accomplishment will ever satisfy you. Once the end result is achieved, the ego will search for something else to attain. In this way you will never be truly happy. The wanting of possessions and circumstances can never fulfill your inner being, because everything exterior is depleting. Nothing lasts forever in the realm of form.

It is right to have goals, but if they are self-indulgent or based on physical possessions, your goals should be reassessed.

Day 248
Anger

"Holding on to anger is like grasping a hot coal with the intent of throwing it at someone else; you are the one who gets burned."

Buddha

Ego loves anger. Because it vibrates at such a high frequency, it will use every opportunity possible to feed itself. Some people have triggers. You will notice they get upset at the slightest irritant. This is not who they are. This is ego. Anger is negative, yet it is higher than lust or fear because it creates an outburst of energy. With the emotion of anger there are feelings of hostility, annoyance, stubbornness, destructiveness, aggression, violence, or rudeness. Large political rallies, fights against a cause, and other such group gatherings give a heightened sense of anger. They are based on the notion that we are right and they are wrong. It feeds the inner drama and unifies large masses of people, only to create more destruction and chaos. In creating opposition, there will always be a feeling of anger or resentment. In this way, peace will never be the outcome.

Let go of the need to be right. In being right you are making someone else wrong. There is no need to be right. Everyone has different views. Why do you need to express yours?

Day 249
Pride

"Pride is an admission of weakness; it secretly fears all competition and dreads all rivals."

Fulton J. Sheen

Pride is the final stage of negative emotion. It is the last step in forgoing the self, yet it is the hardest to move past. With the feeling of pride come arrogance, belief that we know it all, judgments, opinions, selfishness, vanity, snobbery, narrow-mindedness, and gloating. Pride is very close to being positive, as there is awareness that we are unique and gifted. However, pride indicates that we think this power comes from ourselves, and not from a greater source. With pride there is a notion that we are superior to all beings and therefore know better and are better. However, this could not be further from the truth. Many people experience pride, especially people of power. They see themselves as gods or goddesses, but if questioned, deny this fact. If we come to the realization that we are all-encompassing and abundant, the ego will be forgone and positive levels of consciousness will be attained.

Pride is easy to fall into if you have a separatist view. With the belief that there is no God comes pride. Realize we are all God, no matter who we are or what religion we follow. Together we create reality.

Day 250
Courageousness

"God places the heaviest burden on those who can carry its weight."

Reggie White

Courageousness is the epitome of positive emotion. In feeling courageous, you are purposeful, happy, motivated, supportive, giving, a visionary, creative, aware, clear, adventurous, optimistic, and confident. To have courage is to be selfless. People with courage find purpose for their lives and attain goals. It is the realization that everything takes time, but it does not matter how long it will take. It's more about the journey than the outcome in the future. This is the beginning of being present. All positive emotions have significantly more power and energy than negative emotions. One person in the world who is courageous is the equivalent of thousands of people who think negatively and experience low levels of consciousness on a daily basis.

See if any of the above feelings pertain to your experiences. If they do, do more of that. In doing so, you will become more positive and aware.

Day 251
Acceptance

"When you find peace within yourself, you become the kind of person who can live at peace with others."

Peace Pilgrim

For most people acceptance happens in old age, and for many, not at all. Acceptance is the notion that everything simply is and nothing needs to be changed. Your inner and outer being is fulfilled, and a sense of wonder and awe enters your being. Feelings associated with acceptance are childlikeness, compassion, gentleness, intuitiveness, joyfulness, harmony, beauty, consideration, abundance, balance, openness, and radiance. Acceptance happens through the process of letting go and allowing the now moment to be as it is. Only when we continue on the level of courageousness can acceptance be obtained. This level of consciousness is much higher than courage, as it fulfills the destiny of the evolution of consciousness. The human body is created to be a vessel through which consciousness can become aware of itself. Acceptance of the now is this arising.

One cannot force him- or herself to accept the now moment. It must be done effortlessly. The first step is to either accept, enjoy, or be enthusiastic about everything and nothing.

Day 252
Peace

"There is no way to peace; peace is the way."

A.J. Muste

Most people will not experience peace in this lifetime. This is not to say that it is not possible; it just means that they are far from it. With the incessant stream of unconscious negative emotions that has taken over most of today's population, it is a wonder that we will ever obtain such a feat. However, it is our destiny to be at peace and one with the universe. Feelings associated with peace are agelessness, awareness, calmness, understanding of I am, oneness, quietness, spaciousness, fulfillment, purity, perfection, serenity, and completion. One person at this consciousness level is the equivalent of millions of people at lower levels. This is how the world balances itself. However, as more people become aware of consciousness within themselves, the numbers of people who experience peace on earth will rise. People who have experienced this level of conscious awareness include Jesus, Lao Tzu, and the Dalai Lama.

Meditation and inner stillness are the first steps toward peace. Change yourself to change the world. You are already on the right path, because you are reading this book.

Day 253
Numbers

"I think my numbers speak for themselves."

Jack Youngblood

Numbers are significant. Each number from 1 to 9 has a different meaning. Astrology is based on numbers and predictions. Sacred geometry tells us about how numbers are involved in everything. Birth dates show a lot about our natural abilities simply because they are made up of numbers. It is believed that numbers make up everything we see and don't see. They can guide you in the right direction in finding your true calling. Use your birthday to find the number that influences your life the most. For example, March 11, 1981, is broken down as follows: (March is the 3rd month) 3 + 1 + 1 + 1 + 9 + 8 + 1 = 24 → 2 + 4 = 6. The main influence of this birth date is the number 6. There are also four 1's, 3, 9, and 8, which hold secondary meanings. Your time of birth can also be used in certain calculations. The next nine days will deal with the significance of each number, from 1 to 9.

What is the main number influence on your life, dictated by your birth date?

Day 254
1

"The sun illuminates only the eye of the man, but shines into the eye and the heart of the child."

Ralph Waldo Emerson

The symbol for the number 1 is sun. It represents new beginnings. Along with new beginnings come positive action and ambition. Just as the sun radiates its energy on the earth, 1 gives us the energy to move forward and accomplish our goals. It is only fitting that the first number represents the start of something great. One is also seen as being both physical and mental. We are one and complete when we exercise both sides of our being. When right action stimulates our physical and mental nature, we accomplish great things.

Take notice on how the number 1 influences your life.

Day 255
2

"Three things cannot be long hidden: the sun, the moon, and the truth."

Buddha

The symbol for the number 2 is moon. It signifies balance, opposites, and choice. Two is the influence of other people and working with like-minded individuals. This is the process of planning and decisiveness. The number 2 represents duality, such as having to make a choice. Where the number 1 is the sun, 2 is the opposite, moon. Without day you would not have night. The moon's light is a reflection from the sun, and so we are told to reflect or think about our actions. This is why the number 2 signifies planning. We must have balance in our lives and deal with others in a compassionate manner. Two is very important to our interactions with others in the world.

Where do you notice the influence of 2 in your life?

Day 256
3

"Joy is but the sign that creative emotion is fulfilling its purpose."

Charles Du Bos

The symbol for 3 is Mars, and its general meanings are creativity, joy, and intuition. Three also represents the past, present, and future. One is day, 2 is night, and 3 is the continuation of the progression of days and nights passing by. Life is made up of moments, all of which are experienced right now. Three is the joy of living. By being creative and ever present, the number 3 responds to our life by providing the joy of living. Three also recognizes that our outer world is a reflection of our inner being. It is said that if you want to know what you were thinking in the past, look at your body now. If you want to know what your life will be like in the future, look at what you're thinking now. Three is joyous and success driven. It is new adventures alongside cooperation with others.

Does the number 3 have influence on your life? Are you creative and adventurous? Do you experience the joy of now?

DAY 257
4

"Four steps to achievement: Plan purposefully. Prepare prayerfully. Proceed positively. Pursue persistently."

William Arthur Ward

The symbol for the number 4 is Mercury. It represents calmness or Mother Nature. Four is depicted in life as the four seasons, the four elements, and also the four directions: north, south, east, and west. This number means stability, endurance, and nurturing. Those who are influenced by this number either already have or need a stable home life. Four also represents gathering strength. One uses the stability of the earth to gain energy and become more in touch with his or her inner self.

Use the number four anytime you feel lost. Meditate on the number and notice its occurrences in your life.

Day 258
5

"I was trying to daydream, but my mind kept wandering."

Stephen Wright

The symbol for the number 5 is Jupiter. The spiritual meaning of the number is travel, adventure, and motion. Its energy is unpredictable and signifies change. When the number 5 appears in your life, expect to travel, but not necessarily physically. Five can make your mind wander and daydream. Remember the law of attraction—thoughts become things. Make sure that if your mind wanders, you are thinking positive thoughts. It is always best to stay grounded and present. If the number 5 is influencing your life, you may have a tendency to be unhappy with the present. Therefore you daydream about circumstances that have not yet come to pass. Change is great, and is a necessary part of life. However, waiting for change in order to be happy will never work. You can only be happy now.

Are you expecting change in the future in order to be happy? Relax and enjoy the journey now.

Day 259
6

"Only those who have learned the power of sincere and selfless contribution experience life's deepest joy: true fulfillment."

Anthony Robbins

The number 6 is tolerant, sincere, and forgiving. The symbol for 6 is the planet Venus. When you are influenced by this number, sincerity and compassion are your main concerns. In dealing with situations, one always seeks to find diplomacy. The number 6 is said to shed light on a situation and provide inner guidance in a peaceful manner. Six is very spiritual, as it guides a path to enlightenment. This is the great power of the universe, as we are spiritual beings encountering a human experience. The influence of Venus and the number 6 is very important. To be in touch with your inner self serves a purpose for all humanity.

Are you aware of your inner presence? Are you compassionate and forgiving? How does the number 6 influence your life?

Day 260
7

"Magic is believing in yourself; if you can do that, you can make anything happen."

Johann Wolfgang von Goethe

The number 7 represents mystery, magic, and legend. The symbol for 7 is Saturn. Through conscious awareness, 7 helps us to understand the mysteries of the world. It vibrates at a frequency that gives us depth and knowledge in the most profound undertakings. There stands a reason why there are seven wonders of the world. People influenced by the number tend to daydream; however, when applied, this number can turn daydreams into realizations.

Are you a daydreamer? Do you often think about the supernatural? You may be onto something. This is the number 7 at work.

Day 261
8

"Falsehood has an infinity of combinations, but truth has only one mode of being."

Jean-Jacques Rousseau

The symbol for 8 is Uranus. Its meanings are success, strength, and opportunity. If you analyze how the number 8 looks, you will see it is a line that can be followed again and again, creating a circular path. It is in this way that you become successful. When you are determined, you can persevere and perform an action time and time again until you are successful. Eight also represents continuation and cycles. With every ending there is a new beginning. In business or any other venture, there are ups and downs and various cycles. Following trends and continuing your vocation while applying focus will breed success. If you use the number 8 in this way, wealth will certainly come to you not only in the form of materials, but in all aspects of life.

Find your true calling and focus. Ride the cycles of life and prosper as the number 8 influences you.

Day 262
9

"Everything is the product of one universal creative effort. There is nothing dead in nature."

Seneca

The symbol for the number 9 is Neptune, and its meaning is universal influence. This number is the basis for intellectual power and satisfaction in accomplishment. This is the highest vibration of positive awareness, and we are surrounded by its influence. We cannot escape the positive vibrations of the universal influence; to do so leads to self-destruction through negativity and resentment. All numbers above 9 relate to it in some way. Here are three examples:

The number 18: 1 + 8 = 9.

The number 37: 3 + 7 = 10. 37 – 10 = 27. 27 is divisible by 9, or 2 + 7 = 9.

The number 74: 7 + 4 = 11. 74 – 11 = 63. 63 is divisible by 9 and 6 + 3 = 9. Once again, 9 is the number of the universe. Entire books have been written about the number and its vibration frequency.

Do you notice that we are surrounded by a power much greater than ourselves? Can you see how we are all connected? Can you feel the power numbers have on the universe?

Day 263
Auras

"Words were never invented to fully explain the peaceful aura that surrounds us when we are in communion with minds of the same thoughts."

Eddie Myers

We are energy contained in human form. Our bodies are the vessels that allow us to be. Energy has taken many names, such as spirit, light, and aura. An aura is the energy that surrounds the body, radiating out into the world. It is the attractive force that brings like-minded beings into your awareness. It is directly related to your frame of mind and thoughts. Auras change and are said to have colors. There are people who have the ability to see auras, while others are oblivious to them. Regardless of whether you believe in auras or not, the fact is you have one. You are not your body, but rather the energy that emanates from it. It is like a fish not knowing it is swimming in water. The fish is oblivious to it, yet we know water exists. You are conscious awareness. Your aura can be felt and seen by others. Most people do not see them, but they certainly feel auras. The more in touch you are with your surroundings, the more present auras will be to you.

Sit comfortably in dimly lit stillness. Relax and breathe deeply. Take notice of the aliveness that is within you. This energy is your aura.

Day 264
Flower of Life

"Nature is the art of God."

Dante Alighieri

The flower of life (see below) is a circle containing geometrical patterns that relate to all sentient beings. The patterns of the flower of life have been studied by many scholars throughout the centuries. Upon dissecting the images within the flower, people have found it to reflect our level of consciousness in this world. Not only that, but within its patterns lies a blueprint for all beings living on this earth. The flower of life is profound and has been engraved in many ancient stones and hieroglyphs around the world. The images also show us our vibration frequencies and thought patterns that create our reality.

As we grow and evolve, our conscious awareness expands. You are growing and expanding in every moment. Always plant seeds of positivity and gratitude.

DAY 265
INDIGO CHILDREN

"Children are the world's most valuable resource and its best hope for the future."

John Fitzgerald Kennedy

Many children born after the year 1984, and especially around 1999, are said to have a special gift. As the consciousness level of humanity rises, babies being born have a more advanced genetic makeup as opposed to adults born years prior. Indigo children have the ability to see into the future, vivid memories of past lives, increased immune systems, and a heightened awareness. These special children are known to have a blue aura surrounding them. Their powerful senses and views of reality are far superior to what humanity once was. One can attribute this genetic transformation to the constant efforts of humans as we learn and grow. Remember, we are spiritual beings encountering a human experience.

Is it really so hard to believe that humans are evolving? The evidence is all around. Notice how you and those around you are growing with every new day that passes.

Day 266
Chakras

"There is deep wisdom within our very flesh, if we can only come to our senses and feel it."

Elizabeth A. Behnke

The human body is made up of pure energy. Within us are limitless power and potential. Like all things, we vibrate at a frequency. The rate of vibration varies depending on our thoughts and feelings. A chakra is a power source in the body. There are seven main chakras located throughout the body, running from the base of the spine to the crown of the head. These power sources, when open, give us energy, insights, and well-being. Throughout the day these power sources open and close depending on our vibration frequency. Not all chakras are open for all people. Only with practice and clarity of mind will the chakras open to give heightened sense perceptions and awareness. Over the next seven days we will look at each chakra and its function.

Sit in stillness and observe the sensations within the body. Feel the energy and limitless potential of your inner being.

Day 267
Root or Base Chakra

"Our own physical body possesses a wisdom which we who inhabit the body lack. We give it orders which make no sense."

Henry Miller

The color of this chakra is red, and it is located at the base of the spine. The lesson is survival. When a baby comes into this world, the base chakra is the only chakra open. The baby's need for survival is first and foremost. With all chakras, the next cannot be opened until the needs of the one prior to it have been met. When a human is in survival mode, it is a very primal impulse. One must feel secure with his or her surroundings and deal with material tasks in a comfortable manner. Physical exercise and restful sleep aid this chakra. Also, consuming red food and drink is known to stimulate this chakra. Noticeable imbalances include cold hands and feet, fatigue, lower back pain, and depression.

Is your base chakra open or closed? Do you experience any of the imbalances listed above? If so, are you getting enough rest and exercise?

Day 268
Spleen Chakra

"Emotion always has its roots in the unconscious and manifests itself in the body."

Irene Claremont de Castillejo

The second is the spleen chakra, which is located along the spine below the navel in the abdomen area. Its color is orange. Your feelings and emotions are associated with this chakra. Have you ever noticed that when you feel nervous or excited you may get a sensation in the pit of your stomach? This is your spleen chakra wide open. Also associated with this chakra are intimacy and sociality. To stimulate this chakra you may take hot baths, have a massage, or just simply embrace body sensations. Orange food and drink and essential oils also aid in its opening. Noticeable imbalances in the body include eating disorders, drug and alcohol abuse, allergies, asthma, or urinary problems.

How in touch with your feelings are you? Are you open to the senses? Do you embrace your body's natural perception?

Day 269
Solar Plexus Chakra

"No man is free who is not a master of himself."

Epictetus

This yellow chakra is above the navel in the stomach area along the spine. Its attribute is personal power. The solar plexus chakra gives us the right to think, self-confidence, and humor. The ego stems from here, along with our sense of self. Things that stimulate this chakra include taking classes, learning, sunshine, mind games, yellow food and drink, wearing yellow clothes, and detoxification programs. Imbalances in the body that are related to this chakra include constipation, diabetes, poor digestion, ulcers, nervousness, and memory loss.

Are you stimulating your mind on a daily basis? Are you confident yet humble? Do you enjoy learning?

Day 270
Heart Chakra

"Love all, trust a few, do wrong to none."

William Shakespeare

The heart chakra is green and is located in the center of the chest. This is the relationship power source in the body. The right to love and be loved, forgiveness, compassion, self-control, and acceptance are all attributes of the heart chakra. To open this chakra, you can spend time with friends and family or take a walk in nature. Green clothes or green food and drink also help. Noticeable disorders include heart and breathing problems, breast cancer, weak immune systems, muscular tension, and high blood pressure.

Do you share love and compassion with those around you? Do you believe that if you accept your surroundings you will have a decreased chance of high blood pressure?

Day 271
Throat Chakra

"To speak and to speak well are two things. A fool may talk, but a wise man speaks."

Ben Jonson

The throat chakra is blue and is located in the middle of the throat. Like the heart chakra, the throat chakra also has to do with relationships. However, the nature of its power differs in that it focuses more on speech, communication, expression, loyalty, trust, and organization. It makes sense that this power source is where the vocal cords are located. It is important to note that chakras, even though they are said to have a place in the body, really do not take any space at all. They are invisible power regions located along the center of the body. The throat chakra is stimulated by singing, having meaningful conversations, or collecting beautiful works of art. One can also wear the color blue and eat or drink blue food to stimulate this region. You will know the throat chakra is not properly stimulated if you have a thyroid imbalance; there is pain in your mouth, jaw, neck, shoulders, or throat; you have a fever or flu; or you suffer from mood swings.

Do you sing? Your body loves it when you do. Sing today. Do this alone if necessary.

Day 272
Third Eye Chakra

"Intuition is a spiritual faculty and does not explain, but simply points the way."

Florence Scovel Shinn

The third eye chakra is an indigo color and is located between your eyes on your forehead. This is where your intuition comes from. It is in this place we develop our sixth sense and psychic abilities. If this chakra is open fully, you will be more in touch with your true spiritual self and will gain insight and understanding of your true nature. This chakra is stimulated by activities that evoke wonder, such as gazing at the stars or enjoying the beauty of nature. Indigo food and drink are also stimulants. The greatest way to open this chakra is through meditation and calmness of mind. The imbalances of the body which deter from the third eye opening are exactly the same as those associated with the throat chakra. One cannot open the third eye without having first unlocked all previous chakras. This is why in meditation you must completely relax and feel comfortable with your surroundings.

Do you have a natural intuition? Can you sense and feel circumstances that have not yet come to pass? Can you see auras? This is your third eye wide open.

Day 273
Crown Chakra

"Not all those who wander are lost."

J. R. R. Tolkien

The location of the crown chakra is the top of the head, and its color is violet. The attribute of the crown chakra is pure knowingness. This is your connection with God or higher power. Once the crown chakra is reached, new levels of consciousness and vibration frequency are achieved. Through the integration of the conscious and subconscious mind, the human taps into superconsciousness. This is the place where all things are known and understood. To obtain this heightened awareness, one must be extremely balanced and at peace. The crown chakra opens to those who focus on dreams, write down visions and intentions, and follow their hearts. Violet food and drink aid in the preparation for opening this chakra, as well as violet gems and clothing. Malfunctions of this chakra are expressed by constant headaches, mental illness, epilepsy, skin rashes, and photosensitivity.

Maybe now you can see why pursuing your goals is so important. Your happiness and well-being are crucial in obtaining higher levels of consciousness.

DAY 274
IQ

"I know that I am intelligent, because I know that I know nothing."

Socrates

The intelligence quotient is a score given to an individual to reflect the amount of knowledge he or she has. Higher scores indicate better problem-solving abilities, math skills, and common knowledge. However, an IQ test does not reflect consciousness level or how one interacts with others. Nor does it illustrate how giving people are, or if they follow their hearts. On one hand, an IQ test is ideal for showing aptitude and study habits; on the other hand, it is very limiting. Oftentimes we humans like to know how smart we are, or how far along we have come. Why? To compare?

There is no limit to the amount of love we can give or receive, and that is more important than what any IQ test can tell you.

Day 275
Goal Check #6

"The road leading to a goal does not separate you from the destination; it is essentially a part of it."

Charles de Lint

After ten months since you initially set your goals, how far have you come? Have you been taking the little baby steps necessary to attain your greatest dreams? A prime example of attaining a goal is this very book you are reading. Entries were completed regularly, one or two each day. Little by little the individual efforts added up to a great work of art. Remember, the greater the goal, the more it needs to be broken down. You are your biggest challenge. You can do anything and be anything. However, you first have to believe it within yourself.

Take the little steps toward your goals every day. Review and make sure you are on the right track. Follow your heart.

Day 276
The Senses

"Seeing, hearing and feeling are miracles, and each part and tag of me is a miracle."

Walt Whitman

Our senses are the way we perceive reality. Interestingly, everyone has a different view of reality because our senses are different and unique. The senses are vision, hearing, touching, tasting, smelling, and the sixth sense. What is truly fascinating is that if you think about all the things we cannot see, taste, touch, smell, or hear, there are an infinite number of forces that remain unexplored and unexplained. Our senses are truly unique and shape our limited view. Our senses are just the tip of the iceberg. Imagine yourself at the bottom of a well looking up at the sky. You would be able to see only a small portion of a vast world. This is our perception of what truly is. Even though our senses are very powerful, there is still so much we do not know. We were given the unique gifts of the senses, and over the next six days we will explore all their virtues.

Remain aware at all times of the body's natural reaction to situations and circumstances. Your reactions create your reality.

Day 277
Sight

"For my part I know nothing with any certainty, but the sight of the stars makes me dream."

Vincent van Gogh

Our sense of vision is truly magnificent. Without even thinking, we can see thought forms manifested into reality. Looking around, we see beauty as it takes shape in form and formless. Without sight it would be very difficult to live in our reality. Sight alone allows us to easily go from place to place, watching for obstacles that may block our path. Seeing gives us the power to communicate without words, using actions or gestures to convey messages. However, it is sight that limits our view. Our ability to see reality leaves us blind to what we cannot see. Most people have trouble believing in what they cannot see, because they are too involved in the sense of sight. Our eyes are the most precious gift, and our biggest curse. Sight is limiting if we cannot see through the hologram of form.

Take a moment to appreciate the gift of sight. Then realize there is much more you will never see with your eyes.

Day 278
Hearing

"See how nature—trees, flowers, grass—grows in silence; see the stars, the moon and the sun, how they move in silence … we need silence to be able to touch souls."

Mother Teresa

Our ability to hear sounds as they travel through the air is amazing. It is said that when someone loses a sense, the others are heightened. Blind people tend to have a greater sense of hearing, because they use it as if it were their sight. Sounds are vibrations that travel to our eardrum. The tiny hair follicles in our ear move up and down as sound travels in and out. Our brain picks up the frequencies, and our mind deciphers what is going on around us. At any given moment we hear many sounds at the same time, dismissing them for fact as we go through our daily lives. Acoustical vibrations are fascinating. This invisible force moves through the air, undetectable by the eye. Sound and music move the body in creative ways. Our bodies were made to hear and feel sound. We don't just hear with our ears, but with our entire being.

Wherever you are, take a moment to sit quietly and listen. What different sounds do you hear simultaneously? Pay close attention to each sound individually. Notice any slight changes in your body.

Day 279
Touch

"One touch of nature makes the whole world kin."

William Shakespeare

Our sense of touch is very powerful and necessary to our survival. Many studies have been done on infants with regard to the touch of a mother. It has been found that without the affection and warmth of a motherly figure, an infant will grow to have mental disorders and communication dysfunctions. Through touch we feel soft, hard, rough, wet, dry, cold, and hot. What is it that allows us to experience touch? Is it the skin? It is amazing how our bodies experience this sense perception. Sometimes what we feel as hot can seem cold. Or sometimes we get shivers in our bodies from various situations and circumstances. Touch unites us through love and affection toward one another. Touch allows us to feel reality in ways we could never imagine.

With an open mind throughout the day, run your fingers along different surfaces to feel their texture. Does anything come to mind?

DAY 280
TASTE

"All of life is a dispute over taste and tasting."

Friedrich Nietzsche

The human tongue allows us to experience unimaginable sensations of taste. On different parts of the tongue we can experience salty, sweet, sour, and bitter. Our mouths are a very special and vital part of our body. You can tell a lot about a person's health by looking at his or her teeth. To care for your mouth improves your health and longevity, as well as your ability to taste. We also use our mouths to talk and kiss. Have you ever wondered why we kiss as a form of affection? There is a simple reason: because it feels good. The senses of the tongue apply not only to taste, but also to sensual feelings.

When eating anything today, take the time to experience the flavor fully. Enjoy the sensations of the entire piece of food until it is swallowed. Chew slowly.

Day 281
Smell

"Take time to smell the roses."

Proverb

Smells are a big part of who we are. Everyone smells different. In fact, certain animals, such as dogs, use smells to determine their territories, to form their opinions about other animals and people, and to find their way. Smell also has a lot to do with whom you choose as a mate. A smell either attracts you to someone, or repels you. Certain aromas give us body sensations and either calm us or create anxiety. Without even realizing it, we are guided by our sense of smell in ways we cannot even imagine.

Take a moment to smell a beautiful flower today. How does it make you feel?

Day 282
The Sixth Sense

"The sixth sense is at the core of our experiences. It is what makes experiences out of events."

Henry Reed

There is no name to describe this sense perception. To put it simply, this is our awareness of the supernatural. Some people are more open to this concept than others. However you want to think about it, there are external forces acting upon our lives. We know gravity exists, yet we cannot see it. When we are more open to our other five senses, the sixth sense is the next step in transformation. Most people never experience the sixth sense, because of fear of the unknown. However, there is nothing to fear. All fears are only in the mind. What is there to fear if the world is full of love and acceptance? Through fear we limit ourselves. It is believed that the sixth sense is just the beginning to new and evolving conscious awareness.

Do you believe that humans have the ability to sense things outside of the original five senses? Do you think there are unexplored senses we cannot perceive?

Day 283
Einstein

"A person who never made a mistake never tried anything new."

Albert Einstein

Albert Einstein was amongst the greatest scholars the world has ever known. His many contributions to the scientific community and the world at large paved the way for many great inventions and theories. The general theory of relativity was amongst his greatest achievements. It is important to note that Einstein's success did not happen overnight. It took years and years of thinking and theorizing to come up with the amazing works of his time. His lifetime of work is a legacy. It is through his natural love for science, hard work, and dedication that his greatness was achieved.

Einstein's story is illustrated here to provide an inner sense of accomplishment. Even after his greatest theories were published, Einstein still could not find a job, even as a high school science teacher. It takes perseverance and persistence to be someone great. Strive for your inner purpose. It is worth the wait.

DAY 284
MUSCLE TESTING

"What the mind dwells upon, the body acts upon."

Denis Waitley

Your body has the ability to answer any question you can ask it. Find the truth about what allergies you have, how daily habits affect you, or what psychological stress has come from worries and anxieties. The process is actually quite simple and straightforward. Muscle testing can be done alone or with a friend. Lie on your back. Raise your left arm into the air. Your partner stands beside you with his or her index finger placed about three inches back from your wrist. Now, with minimal effort your outstretched arm moves back as the index finger of your partner attempts to push the arm down. Your arm will stay in the air no matter how much pressure is applied from the index finger. Do this a couple of times to get comfortable. Now ask yourself questions. If your name is Peter, say, "My name is Peter." Push back your arm to meet the index finger. The tester will not be able to push down your arm. Now say a lie: "My name is Nancy." When pushing back, your arm will be weak and will go down effortlessly. For this to be accurate, you must be comfortable and in the right environment with no interruptions.

Take a moment to try muscle testing. The results may surprise you.

Day 285
Muscle Test Questions

"The mind commands the body and it obeys. The mind orders itself and meets resistance."

Saint Augustine

Once you get comfortable with muscle testing and have gotten past the point of amazement, it is time to ask your body questions. As a general guide, if you ask a question and your arm stays strong, the answer is positive, meaning your body is fine with whatever you asked. If your arm goes weak, it means your body has a problem. For instance, ask, "Am I allergic to grass?" If your arm goes down, you are allergic to grass, because your body is weak. You could also ask, "Do I have any allergies?" If your arm stays strong, then you don't. If you do have allergies, you can go one step further and ask, "Am I allergic to any kinds of food?" If your arm goes weak, you can then ask about types of food. You will be surprised at the results. Sometimes, bodily dysfunctions come from consuming things we are allergic to without even realizing it.

Have an open mind. Try muscle testing. Your body never lies.

Day 286
Colors

"There are only three colors, ten digits, and seven notes; it's what we do with them that's important."

Jim Rohn

The rays of the sun provide us with light, warmth, and energy. It is because of light that we see colors. Without sun we would not have life. As the sun's rays hit the earth, we see a variety of colors, which vibrate at different frequencies. Brighter colors vibrate at higher frequencies than darker ones. The colors of the rainbow have different meanings for us. Color vibrations are a source of energy. Many people use various kinds of colored stones to provide mental and physical healing. Over the next seven days, we will look into the colors of the rainbow, their individual meanings, and how they make us feel and contribute to our well-being.

Surrounding yourself with specific colors will make you feel different. The color of food you eat, the clothes you wear, and the colored life around you affect your mood and health.

Day 287
Blue

"Blue color is everlastingly appointed by the Deity to be a source of delight."

John Ruskin

Blue is the color of spirituality. It indicates distance, such as in the sky, oceans, and heavens. One only needs to look up on a clear day to see the vastness of the color blue. It helps us to see beyond our physical environment and expand our perceptions. Blue is calm and relaxing, it helps us express ourselves to others, and it gives us peace and understanding.

If you find yourself stressed and filled with anxiety, bring this color into your life to calm your senses. Take deep breaths and relax.

DAY 288
YELLOW

"Some painters transform the sun into a yellow spot; others transform a yellow spot into the sun."

Pablo Picasso

Yellow is associated directly with the sun and provides life energy. Yellow is the color of wisdom. It stimulates the body and lightens our lives. When we are influenced by this color, we experience clarity of mind, improved memory, physical strength, and energy. Yellow stimulates our thoughts and problem-solving abilities. Life grows and evolves, and so do our bodies and minds.

Use the color yellow to enhance your mode of thinking. Its life energy stimulates your inner being and abilities to troubleshoot and provide guidance.

Day 289
Red

"Red is the ultimate cure for sadness."

Bill Blass

Red completes the three primary colors: red, blue, and yellow. Any other color can be made from these primary three. Red symbolizes vitality and has the longest wavelength, vibrating at the lowest frequency of all visible colors. When the spectrum goes past red, it is said to be infrared and thus begins the electromagnetic spectrum. Red makes us active with its vigorous energy. With red we feel energized, passionate, secure, and enthusiastic. When utilizing the three primary colors—red, yellow, and blue—we are balanced in body, mind, and soul. From here we can utilize the secondary colors.

Have you ever seen a bull charge at the color red? It excites the bull as it feels the color's energy and responds. Red is very powerful and invigorating.

Day 290
Orange

"Orange is the happiest color."

Frank Sinatra

Orange sparks creative energy. It is created by combining red and yellow. Together with the energy of red and the wisdom of yellow, one utilizes its magnificent power. When stimulated by this color, one feels creative and playful. It is easy to come up with new and innovative ideas under the stimulus of this color. One can also use orange for practical skills to relieve boredom and obtain equilibrium.

If you ever need new ideas, surround yourself with orange and eat orange foods. This will give you the spark you need to achieve greatness. It doesn't matter whether you believe it or not; just try it.

Day 291
Green

"For in the true nature of things, if we rightly consider, every green tree is far more glorious than if it were made of gold and silver."

Martin Luther

Green is the color of life and nature. One only needs to go outside to see the grass, trees, and plants, to realize the power of this magnificent color. To create green, one combines the mind and spirit, or rather, yellow and blue. In relation to the visible color spectrum, green is in the middle, signifying balance. Because of the placement of this color in the spectrum, the human eye can recognize slight variations of green more easily than with any other color. It is no wonder that money is green, as it also signifies abundance. When influenced by green, one experiences harmony, growth, health, and balance.

To be prosperous and connected, use green. Walk in nature, and take in everything around you. Balance yourself and experience the natural process of growth that green provides.

Day 292
Indigo

"Don't ask what the world needs. Ask what makes you come alive, and go do it. Because what the world needs is people who have come alive."

Howard Thurman

The color indigo represents infinity. It takes the color blue and magnifies it inward. Where blue is the calming vastness of the world, indigo is the bridge to the infinite. As one settles into calmness, eventually there is a point at which the finite becomes infinite. On the opposite end of the spectrum, red is very slow, whereas blue is fast. Indigo is lightning fast. It is interesting to note that the calmer the color, the faster it vibrates. The calmer your mind, the higher your vibration. With indigo one experiences wisdom and self-mastery, and opens a door to the subconscious. Intuition and awareness are heightened, and one also may experience psychic abilities.

Meditation is a basic technique to utilize the power of indigo. The clearer the mind, the closer to indigo vibration one becomes.

Day 293
Violet

"I know that when human beings have learned to control and master matter, thanks to the work of their five senses, they will soar upwards again and start to develop their spiritual senses."

Omraam Aivanhov

Beyond lightning fast is the mastery of the spiritual element, or violet. This is the highest known portion of light visible to the eye. Beyond violet is a new color spectrum unknown to the human. We see the colors red to violet. These are the frequencies we are in tune with on this planet. When balancing our body, mind, and spirit, we can attain higher levels through practice and mind control. Violet is a combination of red and blue, which is the key to unlocking its great mystery. The high intensity of red provides a vital energy to the calmness of blue. With red energy, we can utilize the spaciousness of blue to obtain higher levels of consciousness. Through various forms of indigo, we can heal ourselves and others, provide idealism, and create imagination and inspiration. Humanitarianism, true unconditional love, and compassion are associated with this high vibration.

Your aura is a specific color, which indicates your vibration frequency. Violet signifies the attainment of spiritual, mental, and physical harmony with all that is.

Day 294
Philosophy

"One's philosophy is not best expressed in words; it is expressed in the choices one makes ... and the choices we make are ultimately our responsibility."

Eleanor Roosevelt

Philosophy is the study of matters such as existence, values, mind, knowledge, and reason. This book is very philosophical, as the topics discussed pertain to these matters. Everyone has a different point of view, depending on the topic. The point of philosophy is not to determine what is the right or wrong way of thinking. It is to determine why we behave and think in certain ways. The knowledge attained from reading this material has been for your benefit. We hold deep within us, hidden values and beliefs that were implanted when we were children. Through our experiences and environment, we have gained our own perceptions of reality—some good, some limiting. It is through this philosophical evaluation that hopefully you see for yourself what your limits are. You hold the key to unlocking your true potential. This book is simply a guide.

Are there parts of this book that resonated with you more than other parts? You may want to reread those passages. Or, start the journey all over again when the time is right. The choice is yours.

Day 295
Psychology—Part 1

"Follow that will and that way which experience confirms to be your own."

Carl Gustav Jung

Psychology is the scientific study of animal and human behavior. With various experiments, we see how people react to real-life situations and deduce why we behave in certain ways. One fascinating experiment involved a person in a room strapped to an electrified chair. A subject would be taken into the room and given a list of questions to ask the person in the chair. The subject was instructed to push a button every time the person in the chair got an answer wrong. An electric current would zap the person. Every time a wrong answer was given, the voltage would increase. Shockingly, the people asking the questions would never stop the experiment, no matter how badly the person in the chair was tormented. Eventually, the person in the chair would scream at the top of his lungs, begging that the experiment be stopped. Under no circumstance did the questioner stop. This experiment was repeated thousands of times with the same results.

What does this say about humans on a basic level? Why didn't the person asking the questions stop the experiment when they saw the other person in excruciating pain?

Day 296
Psychology—Part 2

"If you never change your mind, why have one?"

Edward de Bono

At first you may think if you were in the situation described in the previous meditation, you would act differently. However, this is not the case, because under certain circumstances people act without thinking logically. During the experiment, what the person asking the questions did not know was that the person in the chair was an actor. At no time was he ever shocked. The purpose of the experiment was to prove that when a person is given a task, he or she completes it no matter what. This is the reason why killing has been justified in times of war. Soldiers have specific orders from someone else, so they are not at fault. People then stop considering the well-being of others and focus on the task at hand. This means that even if another human being's life is on the line, the person will follow the orders. Why? There is an unconscious need to fit in. People are afraid of failing or of what others think of them. In most cases during the experiment the people never stopped, because they were told to finish the questions.

It is truly a wonder how we ever got this far as a civilization with this kind of selfish behavior. Our regard for others is a reflection of our affection toward ourselves.

Phase V—Expansion

Nature, Continuity, and Worldly Issues

DAY 297
SNOWFLAKES

"Nature is full of genius, full of the divinity; so that not a snowflake escapes its fashioning hand."

Henry David Thoreau

Did you know that if you put an individual snowflake under a microscope, the underlying pattern would be different than that of any other snowflake? Interesting, isn't it? When we see the vastness of a snowfall, the flakes all look uniform and one, yet they are all different in nature. A snowflake has but one purpose: to fall from the sky effortlessly until it hits the earth. One day it will melt and transform to water. Then it will evaporate into thin air. It then forms into clouds until it is ready to return to earth in some form of precipitation. We are like snowflakes, having a cycle of life that is effortless and unique. We have a purpose, and it is to be part of the unified flow of life.

Examine your life objectively. Are you happy? Do you flow effortlessly, providing purpose and substance to those around you?

Day 298
Rain

"The best thing one can do when it's raining is to let it rain."

Henry Wadsworth Longfellow

One of the most calming sounds in the world is rain—the patter as it hits the ground and trees, and the cool sensation it provides. Rain is the source of rejuvenation for all plants and animals. It's amazing how water falls from the clouds in such a unique manner. After a hot, dry spell, a downpour of rain is much needed. You can see the relief in nature when this happens. Plants grow again as they are nourished. Water levels rise and provide clean drinking water for animals. Grass turns a healthy green, and the smell in the air is different. Rain is part of a magnificent life cycle. Enjoy and embrace the rain, just like nature.

The next time it rains, watch and listen. Enjoy the moment of the peaceful downpour. We are made of 70 percent water. It is like we are being sprinkled on the earth.

Day 299
Meditation

"Meditation brings wisdom; lack of meditation leaves ignorance."

Buddha

We have all heard the term *meditation*, but what does it mean and how do you do it? Meditation is stillness of mind and body. It is the process of becoming aware of your aliveness. How is this accomplished? Be aware of one breath at a time. A lot of people do not meditate, while some people do but do not realize it. You can meditate anywhere—at home, while driving, at work, outside, etc. It does not matter where you are; what matters is in your mind. If you are someone with little time and patience, try this simple exercise: Wherever you are, give yourself a moment to be alone. Take a slow, deep breath in and out. While doing this, notice how your body reacts to the inhalation as it expands, and the exhalation as it contracts. If a thought comes into your mind, let it go. The main purpose of this exercise is to not think at all. When you have released all the air, notice the stillness of the body. Take a moment to think of nothing. Be careful—even the word *nothing* is still something. Clear your mind.

The more you practice this, the quieter your mind will become. It takes only a few seconds and can be done anytime. Try it first thing in the morning and periodically throughout the day. You will be surprised at your calmness of mind.

Day 300
Nothing

"If you were to take the empty space from all atoms and particles in the universe, all matter would fit into a stadium the size of the Astrodome."

Bill Bryson

What is the word *nothing*? It is composed of two words: *no* and *thing*. No can be looked at as everything that is not. Wherever we are, we are surrounded by what is not. The empty space that fills a room makes it possible for the room to exist. The sound of silence is present always. What we cannot see is the nothingness that gives birth to all things. And what are things? Things are everything we use the senses to perceive. They are what make up our reality to create our experiences. Things are the result of our conscious awareness as a whole. So to think about nothing is to come to realize the emptiness that surrounds all objects in space.

Look around and notice the empty space that surrounds you at all times. Notice the white page these words are written on.

Day 301
Technology

"It has become appallingly obvious that our technology has exceeded our humanity."

Albert Einstein

In the last fifty years we have grown exponentially in terms of technology. Computers are now a common household item. The Internet connects people all over the world. Television has taken over Western civilization. Automation and machines have increased productivity. With this rise of technology, it is easy to see how our population has increased as well. We are now able to cater to the needs of billions of people at a time to lived sheltered, seemingly happy lives. As technology makes its leap into the twenty-first century, it is evident that most people have cut themselves off from Mother Nature. Cities are overpopulated, with little vegetation. Wastefulness has become the norm. What is really interesting is that if we one day lost all electricity, our technology would be the first to go. What would people do? There would be chaos.

Take a walk in nature and notice its stillness and beauty.

Day 302
Nuclear Weapons

"Weapons of mass destruction"

George W. Bush

For many years presidents have been dictating the downfall of peace and harmony between existing nations. Cold war and arms races have been going on for many years, and it is not until now that we are beginning to realize the pain we have caused. Countless people have died from nuclear war, and many have had to leave their homes due to possible threats. One day there will be no such thing as a nuclear weapon. There are facilities around the world that disarm nuclear bombs and missiles. This is the start of a new era when we have finally noticed our own obsessions with ego and destruction. This new realization will lead to the disarmament of all weapons of chaos as we travel the road to peace and oneness.

Thoughts become things. Try to avoid watching movies and television shows with guns and violence as the predominant theme.

DAY 303
ALONE TIME

"I restore myself when I'm alone."

Marilyn Monroe

Being alone is vital to your inner and outer growth as an individual. No matter who you are or what you do, you must make time for yourself. This does not include time spent with distractions. Take at least five minutes a day to allow for clarity and reflection. This time should be used to clear your mind and to focus on the breath. Some people call this meditation; however, most people are afraid of that word, so we'll call it alone time. It doesn't matter where you are, as long as you will not be bothered. You will find that as you practice this, you will be more alert throughout the day, feel calmer, and begin to notice space around everything. Alone time is crucial, especially if you are around people most hours of the day.

When would be the best time for you to have five minutes to yourself? Make it a daily practice at the same time every day.

DAY 304
SILENCE

"There are times when silence has the loudest voice."

Leroy Brownlow

Have you ever been in a soundproof room? If so, you would notice how loud silence is. As soon as the door is closed, the lack of sound takes over. When we listen to the absence of sound, it focuses our attention on the present moment. To hear the sound of nothing allows space between thoughts. Silence can be heard at all times, even when we're submersed in loud noise. Once you recognize the sound of silence, it can be heard anytime, anywhere. All that needs to be done is to be aware of it. For some people the silence in a soundproof room brings awareness to the ringing in the ears. Focus on this ringing to bring about your awareness.

Find a quiet place—it doesn't have to be soundproof—and for a couple of minutes listen to the lack of sounds that surround you. Can you hear the silence?

Day 305
Blindness

"We are blind and live our blind lives out in blindness."

William Carlos Williams

Have you ever wondered what a blind person sees? How fascinating the world must be, not knowing what things look like. Most people see blindness as a curse, yet it is a gift. Yes, it is easier to be in this world with vision. However, the blind have an automatic heightened awareness, simply because they perceive and imagine all the time. Now picture a blind person all of a sudden being able to see for the first time. What would it feel like to see the world of vision and illusion? A man in his early twenties who was blinded at birth once said, "I never desire vision, because the world is beautiful as it is. You sighted people are so ignorant." He has truly accepted his lack of vision as a gift and realizes that his imagination creates a picture far greater than we could ever comprehend. To be blind and live in our world, you must be fully present at all times.

What would it be like to lose your vision entirely? Be thankful for all that you have. You were given your senses, or lack thereof, for a reason.

Day 306
Aliens

"I don't believe that there are aliens. I believe there are really different people."

Orson Scott Card

What is your stance on life on other planets? Do you think we are the only conscious beings that exist in this universe? The term *alien* seems so far-fetched, it's no wonder most people dismiss this aspect of our lives. Most people have a fear of the unknown. *Alien* simply means someone who is not from this country. Think about this: At night when you look up at the stars, each tiny ball of light is the equivalent of our sun in a different solar system many light-years away. Now look around and notice how many stars you can see with the naked eye. There are billions of stars. Think about the endless possibilities and probabilities of there being life in other solar systems. Think about all the great wonders of our world that are so inexplicable and incomprehensible. Things like the Great Pyramid must have been created by intelligent life far greater than our own.

Is there intelligent life on other planets? There is a far greater chance there is rather than not.

DAY 307
ELECTROMAGNETIC

"At the head of these new discoveries and insights comes the establishment of the facts that electricity is composed of discrete particles of equal size, or quanta, and that light is an electromagnetic wave motion."

Johannes Stark

There are many great wonders in our world that tend to go unexplained. The unknown is foreign territory that only a few dare to tread. However, there is an explanation for some occurrences that are seemingly supernatural. When something is electromagnetic, it means it contains a charge and attracts things to it. Water is a great conductor of electricity. When you combine compounds in the air such as oxygen, and in the natural burning of fossil fuels, there is a chemical imbalance. Now picture the Atlantic Ocean, with its water containing various compounds and elements from coral reefs and other various substances from centuries of human waste. Every so often, something electromagnetic will occur out of nowhere to balance out the chemical imbalances of the earth. A fog will appear and attract to it anything in its path.

Be aware that there are many forces of nature we cannot see. We experience them every day. Reflect on this.

Day 308
Sun

"Yeah we all shine on, like the moon, and the stars, and the sun."

John Lennon

It is interesting when you think that our sun is really just another star in the sky. This ball of pure energy sustains life on this planet by providing the warmth we need to survive. Plant life grows and flourishes, water flows, trees bear fruit, and humans evolve. We are only now beginning to harness the sun's energy. There are limitless possibilities that remain untapped in terms of its potential for man.

On a clear night look up to the sky. See the individual stars and ponder the fact that each of them is a sun billions of miles away. Picture yourself living on a planet with one of those stars being your sun. Now look into the sky and see our sun being just another star in the sky.

Day 309
Birds

"Use what talents you possess: the woods would be very silent if no birds sang there except those that sang best."

Henry Van Dyke

The life of a bird is truly amazing. The average bird, weighing only a few ounces, moves quickly and flies with ease. Birds have families, just like us, and communicate with one another. They do not have jobs, nor do the quarrel over petty circumstances. Birds live in harmony with the earth, taking from it only what they need to survive. They are not wasteful, nor do they compete with one another. Mother Nature provides them with the abundance of life. Birds also sense imminent danger approaching, as well as weather changes. We can learn a lot from birds. They do not try to force life, or change what they are. They accept their lives and just simply are.

Birds are great to watch and enjoy. They are very peaceful and full of life. Take the time to pause and listen to their songs of joy.

Day 310
Goal Check #7

"Glory lies in the attempt to reach one's goal and not in reaching it."

Mohandas Gandhi

What do you have to show for this year that has just passed? Are you any closer to attaining your goals, or have you backtracked? Taking a step back is necessary sometimes. Maybe you needed more schooling to do what you really love? Maybe you needed an internship? Whatever the case, this is not the time to worry. All goals and desires are fulfilled. Everything takes time. There is no rush. You must stay on track. Think of how gratifying it will be when you achieve your heart's desire!

You are magnificent and glorious. The world is yours. Be who you were meant to be and fulfill your legacy.

Day 311
Crop Circles

"I don't mind UFOs and ghost stories, it's just that I tend to give value to the storyteller rather than to the story itself."

Robert Stack

The amazing phenomenon of gigantic geometric patterns created virtually overnight can be seen in farmers' fields across the world. Most crop circles are found within forty miles of Stonehenge in the United Kingdom. Some people think people create crop circles and that they are a hoax. Although humans are learning how to create large shapes in farmers' crops, there is an abundance of unexplained phenomena involving these prophetic works of art. During years of testing, people have found that crop circles emit frequencies that promote life. The crops themselves bend in unimaginable ways, yielding patterns of extreme precision unattainable by any person. One can't help but think these crop circles are messages to us from some external source.

Do you believe in messages sent from external sources? Do you believe in unexplainable things we cannot see? Reflect on this.

Day 312
Death

"I am ready to meet my Maker. Whether my Maker is prepared for the ordeal of meeting me is another matter."

Winston Churchill

There is only one thing you can be sure of in life. You will die. This is an inevitable process of our existence, yet so many choose to ignore it. Many fear death and so push it away. What scares people the most is the unknown. It is that separateness from others that we fear. We are not separate; we are one. Look around—we are surrounded by death. Walk in a forest, and you will see life growing on dead wood. Life is a cycle. It can be viewed as a circle. Death is a new beginning. It leads to greater achievements, heightened awareness, and enlightenment. We are destined to die, but we must first accept it. This realization will help you enjoy life, as every moment is a gift from God. When you are appreciative of your gift, new worlds of opportunity will open to you.

Death is a transformation. We are a part of nature and everything else in the universe. We are spiritual beings who live forever. Can you feel that deep down you already know this?

Day 313
Allergic Reaction

"I used to wake up at four in the morning and start sneezing, sometimes for five hours. I tried to find out what sort of allergy I had but finally came to the conclusion that it must be an allergy to consciousness."

James Thurber

Peter loves his spider and takes great care of it. One day he noticed the spider acting weird. It would spend copious amounts of time in its water bowl. Peter decided to take the spider out of the cage and set it down on the table. Upon closer inspection he noticed black mites crawling all over the spider. He put the spider back in its cage, washed his hands, and started to worry. Peter began scratching himself in random places, thinking the mites were on his body. His mind took over, and he made himself sick. He was worried for his well-being.

It is the mind that runs wild. It is up to you to keep it under control. Your reality is a reflection of what you think.

Day 314
Electricity

"Imagination has brought mankind through the dark ages to its present state of civilization. Imagination led Columbus to discover America. Imagination led Franklin to discover electricity."

L. Frank Baum

What an amazing invention. Electricity is one of the most life-changing ideas for humanity in our history. When we walk into a room, all we need to do is turn on a switch and the entire room is illuminated. This is simply fascinating, and yet we take it for granted. Imagine life without electricity. How would your life be different? The first thing that comes to mind is the lights not turning on. What about the storage of food in a fridge? How about that computer you use every day at work and at home? The little electronic devices around the house, like the alarm clock, toaster, dishwasher, and clothes dryer, all use electricity. Our bodies use an electric current to pump the heart. Electricity is within us and around us.

You don't need to know how electricity works to appreciate its novelty. Just look around and see how we are dependent on it.

Day 315
Prayer

"Pray as though everything depended on God. Work as though everything depended on you."

Saint Augustine

Everyone prays, whether you believe it or not. Prayer takes many different forms. People often think of religion when they think of prayer. However, a prayer doesn't necessarily have to do with religion at all. To pray is to speak to God. Usually in a prayer we are asking for something. You may say, "I don't believe in God, so how can I be speaking to it?" Well, you don't have to believe in gravity, but it exists. We are God. When you speak or think, you are always speaking to God, because it is within you and around you. When we ask for things, we are praying. Everyone prays differently. It all depends on your beliefs and values. The more you believe in something, the stronger the prayer.

Try to recall an instant when you prayed, either directly or indirectly. If you cannot, try praying right now. Have an open conversation with yourself.

DAY 316
VISUALIZATION

"Visualize this thing that you want, see it, feel it, believe in it. Make your mental blueprint, and begin to build."

Robert Collier

Visualization is a process by which one pictures a desirable event taking place. The purpose of this exercise is to utilize the power of the mind to attain specific goals and desires. Visualization works on the basis that the subconscious mind does not know the difference between a thought and reality, because everything is thought. The difference with reality is that it is thought manifested into form. To visualize you must completely relax the body. Close your eyes and breathe deeply. Now picture in your mind an event that you would like to experience as if it were happening right now. What do you see? What do you hear? How do you feel? The more vivid the picture, the more real it seems to the mind. Repetition on a daily basis is necessary for visualization to work.

Choose a goal to visualize. Make it something personal. Picture it every day as if it is already accomplished. Your thoughts will be manifested.

Day 317
Autosuggestion

"Your ability to use the principle of autosuggestion will depend, very largely, upon your capacity to concentrate upon a given desire until that desire becomes a burning obsession."

Napoleon Hill

Words are a very powerful tool. We use them every day to communicate with one another to convey our thoughts and feelings. What do you think is the mental makeup of a person who constantly swears and is negative? Do you think this person is generally happy, or depressed? Now think of someone who is positive, outgoing, and accepting. Do you think he or she is happy, or depressed? The point here is that our words are very important to our mental well-being. Autosuggestion is the process by which you listen to positive messages on a daily basis in order to change your way of thinking. Autosuggestion rids the mind of limiting beliefs and negative thoughts. How we think is reflected in our personality, physical appearance, and prosperity. You must change your subconscious way of thinking before your external world will change.

Always make sure you are repeating positive thoughts in your head. Your voice should always be constructive and uplifting. Be aware of your thoughts.

Day 318
Telepathy

"Evidence of clairvoyance, telepathy, or whatever, are not eccentric, isolated instances occurring in man's experience, but are representative of natural patterns of everyday behavior that become invisible in your world because of the official picture of behavior and reality."

Jane Roberts

Telepathy is the ability to communicate with others through thought forms. This is an extremely advanced form of communication, which most humans never experience. However, there are some who do. In fact, there are entire species living on earth that communicate solely through telepathy. Did you know that ants have an exoskeleton body, can lift ten times their weight, and communicate through thought? They are simply amazing creatures. Sometimes we experience moments of telepathy when we can tell what someone is thinking. Usually this is from facial expressions. Also, identical twins have been known to experience communication with one another over long distances. This may be partly due to how connected they are to one another from birth.

Have you ever experienced an instant when you knew what someone was thinking? How about when someone was in danger? This is telepathy.

Day 319
Energy

"Passion is energy. Feel the power that comes from focusing on what excites you."

Oprah Winfrey

Everything is energy. As humans we have limitless potential; we just need to learn how to tap into it. Things vibrate so that we see them as colors and shapes. Some things vibrate at such high frequencies that we cannot see them. We are pure divine energy. Picture the sun, in all its beauty. The sun is a star that burns continuously, providing us with life. We are all part of the sun's energy. We radiate a force field around ourselves. What makes our energy grow and shrink? Love. As we radiate pure love, our energy and consciousness grow to new heights. We become one with our surroundings and cultivated energy. This energy comes from both the sun and Mother Earth.

We are energy fueled by unconditional love. Tap into your abundant energy, and awaken your inner spirit. Feel love and compassion for all beings.

DAY 320
HOLOGRAM

"We are our own creators made, or making ourselves, in the image and similitude of the one Creator. Indeed, since in a hologram the part contains the whole, we *are* the one Creator."

Sol Luckman

A hologram is an image that looks three-dimensional and real. However, upon further inspection we find that it is only an illusion. When looking at a hologram from different angles, we can see it is in fact not a three-dimensional object at all. It is our eyes and brain that play a trick on us. There are many different kinds of optical illusions in our world. Magicians make a career out of this type of trickery. There is a theory that says the entire world is an optical illusion. We think it's real, but what is real? Some believe that our dreams are more real than this reality. It is interesting to think that what has been manifested as form is just a combination of all human imagination. Then, when you sleep, the only imagination existing is your own. Maybe this is how we achieve our dreams? When the thought is powerful enough, it becomes form. If enough people believe something, then it is true in our collective imagination. Thus it becomes real.

Is the world a hologram? Is it a combination of all conscious being's imagination? Reflect on this.

Day 321
Instincts

"Follow your instincts. That's where true wisdom manifests itself."

Oprah Winfrey

Deep within the root of our being we have instincts. Instincts are our true nature and are always right. Animals are so well connected with nature that they always follow their instincts. They thrive with the knowledge of changing weather, how to ensure their survival, and the whereabouts of food and nutrition. We too possess these great qualities; however, most of us never use them. Instincts are a skill; if they are not properly exercised on a regular basis, we lose them. Most often people get caught up in daily routines and neglect their instincts altogether. Your instincts are never wrong. It is your beliefs and deep-rooted issues that cloud your perceptions.

The next time you feel inclined to do something out of the ordinary that is positive, do it. Do not hesitate. These are your instincts.

Day 322
Miracles

"I am the miracle."

Buddha

Miracles are happening all around us every day. All that you need to do to see them is open your eyes. Look around and see the virtue of the physical world. Babies are born every day, flowers blossom, butterflies flap their wings. We are living, breathing miracles. It is a wonder how we got here and how this is happening. To deny the existence of higher power is naive and selfish. Seeing miracles requires the ability to let go. Appreciate and experience the joy of living. We are the miracle, through and through. We are divine essence. What miracle is there to experience if no one is there to witness it? This is the beauty of the human being. Our awareness is the miracle. Our witnessing of the unfolding of nature's beauty is our true purpose. To be blind to this is the downfall of our species.

Live the gift of miracles. See yourself as the miracle, the breath of life.

DAY 323
WATER DROPLETS

"We never know the worth of water till the well is dry."

Thomas Fuller

There is an empty spoon. Using a water dropper, you place drips of water one at a time on the surface of the spoon. As the drops are placed, something interesting happens. The water binds together to form one seamless body of water. Just a minute ago the water was separated by being in the spoon and in the dropper. Now, they come together with no effort. This is who we are. We are made up of mostly water. Our souls are contained within our physical bodies. We are all connected. We are like the raindrops on the ocean, becoming one with all that is. There is not separateness, even when we are unconnected. We transform like water. We will always be part of all that is.

Know that even in our darkest times of disconnectedness, we are still a part of something magnificent.

Day 324
Weather Story

"A cloudy day or a little sunshine has as great an influence on many constitutions as the most recent blessings or misfortunes."

Joseph Addison

Three men went on a road trip to New Jersey to see NASCAR for the weekend. When they arrived it was raining. As they walked to the speedway, they talked about how the cars would not drive in the rain, or even if the track was a little wet, because it was not safe to do so. This did not let them down. In fact, their spirits brightened. Over and over again they kept repeating and singing, "Sunshine, sunshine, sunshine." They even went to the point of making a fake newscast: "This just in: The sun has come out, and the cars are ready to go!" They were having so much fun with the idea of sunshine that they lost track of their surroundings. By the time the announcer called, "Gentlemen, start your engines!" not only was there sun, but the skies were cloudless. It was a beautiful hot afternoon of racing.

We are connected to weather. We are connected to all that is. Our thoughts become things.

Day 325
Oil

"Across the country, people are willing to tighten their belts and sacrifice. The president should ask the oil industry to do the same."

John Salazar

They should coin this era *The Oil Age.* Everything we use on a daily basis requires oil to exist. The most obvious are the cars we drive. Petroleum and the internal combustion engine use oil as their lifeblood. Now think about manufacturing facilities that have long assembly lines with machines working twenty-four hours a day, seven days a week. All those machines require oil to be built and operate. The houses and buildings we use have been erected thanks to oil. Products such as plastic are made from oil. Now think about the damage we are doing to the planet because of our need for this natural resource. Millions of gallons of oil and carcinogens are pumped into the air and oceans every day. There are hundreds of elements in the periodic table. Why do we rely on oil so heavily? Now is the time to be aware of our actions. We must change our ways before it is too late. Mother Earth knows how to balance itself. If that means eliminating the human species, then so be it.

Be aware of how oil products surround us. The first step begins with you. We need creative solutions to our worldly issues.

DAY 326
INSECTS

"We hope that, when the insects take over the world, they will remember with gratitude how we took them along on all our picnics."

Bill Vaughan

It is unfathomable to think of how many species of insects there are. Imagine a world without insects. At first you may think it is wonderful. Then the true notion of interconnectedness sinks in. Without insects, no other life would be possible. There is a statistic that says if bees become extinct the world would end within four years. Some think it would be sooner. If bees were nonexistent, flowers would not be pollinated. Plant life would eventually die out, and larger animals would have nothing to eat. It would only be a matter of time before humans would no longer have food on the planet. This is just one example of many. It is important to note that insects would never completely become extinct. Certain species may come and go, but insects in general have been around for millions of years. Humans have only been here for over one hundred thousand years.

When we realize the importance of the smaller creatures, we can see how insignificant our life issues really are.

Day 327
The Physical World

"The world is not dangerous because of those who do harm but because of those who look at it without doing anything."

Albert Einstein

Have you ever seen a map of the physical world? It is much different than a map of the world as we know it. The physical world shows all the various gradations and surfaces of the planet. On this map there are no such things as countries or boundaries, only different topical land formations. Picture the entire world with no separation, no names or man-made laws. This is the world as God intended, beautiful and magnificent. To live on earth is a privilege overlooked by most. We are constantly creating boundaries and giving names to places. Private property is the name of the game. It seems absurd to think we own a piece of land. Not only this, but we own a piece of land on a property owned by a government. We pay taxes for something that is not really owned by anyone in the first place. This has now become common and is never given a second thought.

Our only limitation is our own behavior. We can never own something much greater than ourselves. We can, however, be a part of it.

DAY 328
REINCARNATION

"As is their awareness, so is their way. According to the account of our actions, we come and go in reincarnation."

Sri Guru Granth Sahib

Do you believe in past lives? How about future lives? Where do you think we go when we die? It is seemingly impossible to think we have not lived before as another being. How could it not be possible? The signs of life and death are all around us. Spirit is forever. Our time here as humans is short in comparison to the existence of all that is. One hundred years is the blink of an eye as compared to the millions of years this planet has been in existence. Humanity is involved in a learning experience. All situations are meant as a test of will and faith. Every moment of every day is lived now. This now moment is your test. Your acceptance of what is, is much more important than any human can comprehend. There are no such things as past and future when all we have is now. Reincarnation is just another passageway into a new learning experience.

Just as we humans grow and evolve, so do our spirits. Different life form energies allow us to be and learn.

Day 329
Is the Jar Full?

"To be full of things is to be empty of God. To be empty of things is to be full of God."

Meister Eckhart

A psychology professor is giving a lecture to a class of students. He shows them an empty jar. He asks the class, "Is this jar empty?" To which they shout out, "Yes!" The professor proceeds to place big rocks in the jar, filling it up to the top with about four rocks. He then asks the class, "Is the jar full or empty?" A couple of students yell out, "It's full!" The professor pulls out smaller pebbles and pours them into the jar, filling in all the gaps between the big rocks. He asks the class again, "Is the jar full now?" "Yes!" the students exclaim laughingly. Finally, the professor pulls out a bag of sand. He proceeds to pour the sand until the granules fill the empty spaces between the rocks and pebbles to the top of the jar. "Now is the jar full?" "Yes," the students reply in disarray. "You are now correct; the jar is indeed full," the teacher concludes.

What is the significance of the rocks, pebbles, and sand in the jar?

Day 330
Empty Jar Explanation

"Self-image sets the boundaries of individual accomplishment."

Maxwell Maltz

Picture the empty jar as your life. The large rocks are your major attainments and accomplishments, such as your house, car, career, and family life. The pebbles signify the smaller aspects of your life, such as hobbies, friends, social events, exercise, schooling, and projects. The sand represents the little things, such as daily routines and habits, experiences, worries, conversations, and spare time. In order to have a completely balanced life, you must acquire equal amounts of rocks, pebbles, and sand in your jar. If you fill the jar with only sand, you will be missing the very important aspects of a successful sustainable living. Likewise, if your jar is filled with only rocks, life will seem empty and meaningless because of the lack of enjoyment and activity.

What do you think your jar would look like? Do you have a fine balance between rocks, pebbles, and sand?

Day 331
The Bible

"May the God of hope fill you with all joy and peace in believing, that ye may abound in hope through the power of the holy Ghost."

Romans 15:13

By far the most influential book ever written is the Bible. Many people have lived and died by the words written in this profound work of art. The most common mistake people make is to take the words written literally. After so many translations and edits, there is no way to interpret its meaning to the fullest potential. We must treat every word with a grain of salt. There are deeper meanings and connotations that lie within its writings and teachings. A lot of people take the Bible to the extreme and cause much pain and anguish. This prophetic book must be looked upon for what it really is: writings and teachings from many authors. It is like looking at a painting and interpreting its meaning. The outcome will be different for each individual. This is how we must come to view the Bible, as an experience for the soul.

There have been many manipulations of faith over the centuries using the Bible. There is much good in its word, but it must be utilized correctly.

Day 332
Pollution

"If not you, then who?"

Hillel

There is only one cause for pollution in the world: humans. We are the reason for the burning of fossil fuels, and the production of carcinogens, toxins, garbage, etc. We are wasteful and diseased. When will we ever learn to not harm Mother Nature? The signs are all around us. Many talk about solving the world's problems, yet few do little. We continue to run factories that create plastic and refine oil. When will it end? We are smarter and greater than this. The answers are all around us. Yet we dismiss the hidden treasures and continue in a downward spiral. It is up to us as individuals to choose right from wrong. To be aware of one's own negligence: To be an advocate of pure natural resources.

You have the ability to change the world. Know that you can do anything. You have the ability to create harmony, or destroy beauty. Be the solution, not the problem.

Day 333
Seeds

"Anyone can count the seeds in an apple, but only God can count the number of apples in a seed."

Robert H. Schuller

The laws of nature are wondrous and awe-inspiring. Within every living organism is the ability to reproduce thousands of times over again. Take, for instance, a plant. First, it starts out as a seed and breaks open. The roots plant deep into the earth's soil. Then, once a firm foundation is acquired, the seedling sprouts upward. Eventually, the plant penetrates the soil to see the light of day. Soon it will blossom into a magnificent creation of nature. Many seeds can be extracted from this plant to re-create its existence over and over again. This is life. We grow exponentially. Our minds, bodies, and souls rise to higher and higher levels without effort. It is the law of the universe to grow forever upward and outward.

There is no undesirable outcome to the mind of God. Everything just simply is.

Day 334
Altruism

"What we have done for ourselves alone dies with us; what we have done for others and the world remains and is immortal."

Albert Pike

Altruism is the practice of unselfish concern and devotion toward other people. Only when we can come to understand and sincerely care for the welfare of others, will we experience inner peace and joy. The more we think of only ourselves, the more depressing and lacking the world becomes. Altruism is the key to harmonious living in the ever-changing cycle of life. In order to survive we must cultivate altruism not only in humans, but also in Mother Nature. Our selfless loving compassion is the one element that can preserve our species' existence on this planet. It is negligence and selfishness that deteriorate the beauty of all that is. Look around and appreciate what has been manifested in order to preserve the wealth of future generations.

Your willingness to cultivate compassion for others is far more important than anything in this world. Love and compassion for all beings are necessary to our survival.

DAY 335
TOILETS

"All perceiving is also thinking, all reasoning is also intuition, all observation is also invention."

Rudolf Arnheim

We take a lot of things for granted; for instance, the toilet. You may be sitting on one right now while reading this. It wasn't that many years ago that there was no such thing as a toilet. Imagine having to go outside every time you needed to go to the bathroom. We are very fortunate to have such a great invention. Another point to consider is that someone invented the toilet. Imagine yourself as the inventor of the toilet. You would be very wealthy. Within you is the key to a great idea. Maybe you can think of a way to improve the toilet. Whatever the case may be, it is something to think about. Every day, we use this marvelous invention many times and never think twice about it. You can accomplish great things, even in the world of feces. You can be number one in the number two business.

Look around at all the amazing ideas. We use them every day and take them for granted. Do you have an idea of your own?

Day 336
Antibiotics

"The trouble with being a hypochondriac these days is that antibiotics have cured all the good diseases."

Caskie Stinnett

The medical profession has advanced in leaps and bounds over the last couple of decades. It is a wonder how we ever survived with the little knowledge we had about medicine. As bacteria and viruses become stronger, scientists create different antibiotics to combat the effects of terminal diseases. When antibiotics were first introduced, the world thought we had a creation that would stop bacteria and viruses completely. What the medical profession did not realize is that the organisms would mutate and become immune to the remedy. This meant different variations of antidotes would be needed to combat multiple forms of disease. Without knowing it, we were creating more disease organisms. Not only this, but the organisms were getting stronger. Today, there are many types of vaccinations and preventative methods to keep people healthy. As we learn more about disease, we see that illness has more to do with a person's mind than a dysfunction of the body.

Be aware of your thinking. Eliminate fear, and you will be healthier and stronger.

DAY 337
HOLISTIC MEDICINE

"The doctor of the future will give no medicine."

Thomas Edison

What seems like a new practice has recently gained mainstream popularity. Natural and holistic medication is quickly becoming the preferred doctoral practice for patients. Through muscle testing, acupuncture, energy transference, and natural herbs and remedies, holistic doctors are taking over the role of family physician. However new it may seem, holistic medicine has been practiced for thousands of years. Nature has within it every conceivable antidote necessary to combat even the most fatal diseases. Your body knows what is best for you, and muscle testing proves it. Your body is an intelligent organism that understands language and has the ability to show when something is not right with its internal functionality. Natural remedies are a great way to cure longtime ailments that have plagued the body and hindered performance without our realizing it. Our bodies know more than we could ever comprehend; all we need to do is ask the right questions.

If you have a disorder or experience any type of pain in your body, you may want to consider a holistic medical practitioner. Your body knows how to heal itself naturally.

DAY 338
ARTHRITIS

"Use it or lose it."

Jimmy Connors

Many people suffer from arthritis. This occurs when we have inflammation in the joints, causing pain and discomfort. For most people, arthritis is at its worst in the morning. This is because we have slept and remained relatively stationary for an entire evening. A lot of people think that arthritis is a disease for old people. This is not true; it can happen to anybody. One of the leading causes of arthritis is not stretching properly. This is why it is most common in older people. They are not very active throughout the years, and so as they age, their bodies seize up and the joints become inflamed. Regular exercise and proper stretching are great ways to prevent arthritis. Our bodies need physical action to sustain healthy, pain-free living.

There is no substitute for regular exercise, a healthy diet, frequent meditation, and Yoga. Your body will thank you.

Day 339
Cancer

"An estimated one out of every four Canadians is expected to die from cancer."

Canadian Cancer Society

Everyone knows someone who has died of or suffers with cancer. The fact is we all have cancer cells lying dormant in our bodies. For some people these cells become active for whatever reason. Did you know that cancer is the most profitable disease in the world? It makes you wonder, if we had a cure, would we know about it? It is like the electric car. The first car ever invented was electric. Then the internal combustion engine came along and changed everything. Any new non-oil-based inventions from that point on were bought by petroleum and oil companies to prevent their products from becoming obsolete. Sometimes money is not always the best answer for coming up with solutions. Oftentimes greed distorts perceptions.

When humans are extinct from planet earth there will be no money. When will we see the harm we are causing to our species and the planet?

Day 340
The Internet

"The Internet is becoming the town square for the global village of tomorrow."

Bill Gates

It is difficult to think of what life would be like without the Internet, yet not too long ago this was a reality. It is truly amazing how computers have connected and united the world. Within a few short years, the Internet has made the world into a very small place. In seconds one can connect and have a conversation with someone from across the globe. Technology has given rise to a new era of forethought and compassion. In this ever-growing populous of machinery, one must remain connected to being human. This means to cultivate inner spirit and awareness of all living things. With technology being so advanced, it's easy to lose focus on the truly important. The Internet helps us connect with one another. It's up to us to fill in the gaps.

In utilizing technology, we should be able to solve the worldly issues that threaten our survival, such as global warming, burning of fossil fuels, and hunger.

DAY 341
HUNGER

"Poor nations are hungry, and rich nations are proud; and pride and hunger will ever be at variance."

Jonathan Swift

Every day, billions of people live without proper nutrition or fresh drinking water. Why are we so fortunate? Most of us were born into families that were financially stable enough to live in a house and afford food and clean drinking water. It is a completely different story for third-world countries. About a third of the world lives in poverty. It is important to be aware of these statistics to better understand why this is happening. No one should have to live on a basis of day-to-day survival when there is infinite abundance in the world. There is more than enough for everyone. All we need is the right frame of mind. We will never advance as a civilization unless we all unite and solve these issues that plague our existence. How is it that we can land on the moon, yet we cannot solve world hunger?

Billions are starving right now and will continue to do so until something is done. What can you do about hunger?

Day 342
Global Warming

"The facts are there that we have created, man has, a self-inflicted wound through global warming."

Arnold Schwarzenegger

The average temperature of the world is rising. As we burn fossil fuels and create pollution, the atmosphere of the earth is becoming denser. As this happens heat from the earth, instead of escaping into outer space, is reflected back onto the planet. This creates stagnation and smog. It is as if our planet is a giant lung and Mother Earth is a chain smoker. Because of our way of life, coral reefs are dying, forests are being chopped down, and polar ice caps are melting. If this continues, the glaciers at the North and South Poles will melt. Water levels will rise and demolish many cities. Air will be so polluted in rural areas that people will not be able to go outside. Plants will no longer grow. Millions of species of animal will become extinct. Scientists are creating alternate ways of living. Natural sources of energy such as wind and sun make it possible to live on our planet without consuming in the way we currently do. There is always a better way to live. We just need to realize the harm we are creating.

Have you ever thought about living differently in terms of consumption? Are there ways you could be more eco friendly in your day-to-day lifestyle?

Day 343
Children

"Truly wonderful the mind of a child is."

George Lucas

What are children to us? They are our equals. Just because someone is younger does not make him or her any less important. Yes, it is true, the child may not know as much as the adult in terms of our reality. But this is simply because of a lack of experience. They are living souls, a part of all that is. In fact, in a way a child is a wise teacher. Every day, children effortlessly use their imaginations freely and enjoy the fascinations of this world. As we grow older, we lose that sense of awe. It is only when we regain the innocence of childhood that we experience true joy and peace. In a lot of ways, adults must learn to be like a child. However, most adults retain the negative aspects of being a child as they grow up; that is, lack of responsibility, selfishness, and neglect. A true inner child is thoughtful, compassionate, and caring. They have wisdom, foresight, and gentleness. People who are true children at heart are happy with the now moment.

We can learn a lot from children. Children can also learn a lot from us, but they can teach us the greater lessons of life.

Day 344
Believe

"Believe and act as if it were impossible to fail."

Charles F. Kettering

You must have complete faith in yourself. Trust in the fact that you are on the right path. Feel yourself becoming more powerful with every new day. Believe that your time will come. You must persevere and be strong. At times it may seem difficult or unclear. Adversity plays a role in everyone's life at one time or another. You must be steadfast and upright. Remain calm, and be thankful for the achievements you have made. Within you is greatness. You are pure, divine, and perfect. You are one with all that is and ever was. You are truly magnificent.

You must believe in yourself to achieve success. Have faith that you can accomplish anything.

Day 345
Winter Solstice

"Winter is the time of love and of taking the light within."

Terry Lynn Taylor

December 21 is the shortest day of the year. For a three-day period the earth is the farthest away from the sun in its yearly cycle. It is during this period that most people commit suicide. The winter solstice is a time of inner reflection. Those who are weak grow weaker. Those who are strong grow stronger. It is said that Jesus died and was resurrected in three days. Jesus was the son of God. Our sun is said to die on December 21 or 22. Three days later, on the day marking the birth of Christ, December 25, the sun is reborn. This is why Christmas is celebrated. It is the birth of our sun, and we now return closer to it on our yearlong journey. For thousands of years civilizations have worshiped the sun. Why not? It is the reason for life on our planet, is it not?

The sun affects us in every way. This is a time of reflection and contemplation. We are the exact distance we need to be from the sun to sustain life on our planet. It really is truly fascinating.

DAY 346
CHRISTMAS

"At Christmas play and make good cheer, for Christmas comes but once a year."

Thomas Tusser

Oh, what a joyous time of family and friends, laughter and singing. For most, Christmas is a time of relaxation and fun. For some, this holiday can be very lonesome. The people who have families are fortunate. Even if you do not get along with your family members, you are still very fortunate. Your family was given to you for a reason. Whether you know this reason or not is a different story. Whatever the case, Christmas is a time of celebration. It is a time of rebirth. We are now on a yearlong journey of exploration and growth. What better way to celebrate than with those closest to us? Over the years this holiday has become very commercialized. Many take for granted its true significance. Be happy with who you are and what you have accomplished.

Enjoy your time with loved ones, and commemorate another year of life. This is the joy of living.

Day 347
War

"War. What is it good for? Absolutely nothing."

Edwin Starr

There has never been a good outcome from war. When we fight with others, it is a time of sorrow and pain. Even victory should be conducted as a funeral. There should be no celebration in the killing of others. Our self-limiting beliefs have created destruction and chaos around the world. Violence, vengeance, selfishness, and ignorance are all by-products of war. Compassion and kindness are the opposites of this mind-set. It is not the birds, nor the animals, nor the trees, nor the oceans that tell us to fight one another. It is us. We are the cause of our own pain and suffering. We segregate and manipulate. We worship false idols and follow crooked leaders. We are our own worst enemy. It is not until we all think independently yet compassionately that war will cease to exist.

Change your thinking. Change your beliefs. Live harmoniously with your brothers and sisters. Peace begins with you.

Day 348
Final Goal Check

"How am I going to live today in order to create the tomorrow I'm committed to?"

Anthony Robbins

As the year comes to a close, it is time to evaluate your progress. Think about your mind-set at the beginning of the year. Think of how far you've come. Look at your goals from January. How do they compare to where you are now? How have you advanced? Are you any closer to your desired outcome? What steps have you taken? You create your own destiny. You must be diligent in creating your path. This is a time to reflect and look toward a new year, to move forward and progress. Your goals are only the beginning of a new life of prosperity and happiness.

Your goals are a reality. You have the power to do anything and become anything. No goal is too high. Keep dreaming. Keep growing and learning.

Phase VI—Wisdom

Poetry and Revelation

Day 349
Keys and Doors

"The world is all gates, all opportunities, strings of tension waiting to be struck."

Ralph Waldo Emerson

Plenty of keys, not enough doors;

You will find your way.

Not enough keys, too many doors;

You will be lost.

Open the door that interests you.

Enjoy and be happy.

Keys are your talents. Doors are your opportunities. Interests are your virtues. Enjoyment is your enlightenment.

Day 350
The Role of Humanity

"Do not worry about holding high position; worry rather about playing your proper role."

Confucius

The role of man is like this:
Observation, circumstance, outcome.

With observation, watch and listen.
Wait and be patient.
Admire your surroundings.

Circumstance: Pursue the interest.
Live the moment.
Remain considerate.

With the outcome, discouragement is not an option.
Every observation is a new circumstance,
A new outlook, a new achievement.
Outcome is never according to plan.

Be humble, be courteous, be last.
You are below all others; remember this.
For you are merely a mortal: Flawed and imperfect.
Filled with divine spirit: Pure and perfect.

The breath of life: A precious gift.
To whom do I owe my undying gratitude?

Be grateful for all you have and do not have. We are here to experience the joy of life.

Day 351
Impermanent

"Everything flows and nothing abides; everything gives way and nothing stays fixed."

Heraclitus

From dust we are born; To ash we return.
However impermanent it may seem.
We are the dirt under the boot;
The water in the sea;
The fire burning with desire.

This gift of knowing and being.
How precious and fragile.
How beautiful and inspiring.
How perfect, yet deceiving.

However impermanent it may seem.

The only reason why we see the impermanence of the world is because we are forever eternal. Reflect on this.

Day 352
Inner Light

"Presence is more than just being there."

Malcolm S. Forbes

Light the way with your presence;
How can this be so?

Desires few and self far gone;
Your light radiates outward.

Where to go from here?
Good intention and compassion;
The way will be lit from a distance.

Your presence is felt by all. You are infinite and perfect. Use your inner light as a beacon of hope and compassion.

Day 353
Unconditional Love

"Intense love does not measure; it just gives."

Mother Teresa

Talk to Him as if it were your best friend;
Openly and with sincerity.

Listen to Him as if it were whispering;
Intently and with the entire body.

Feel Him like a warm blanket;
A shield providing inner warmth.

Follow Him as if it were leading;
Your intuition knows no bounds.

Love Him as if it were your mother;
Unconditionally.

For this is what you are and always will be.

Unconditional love has no opposite. You have purpose. Your life holds meaning. Love yourself and be loved.

Day 354
Calm Emotion

"Power is so characteristically calm, that calmness in itself has the aspect of strength."

Edward G. Bulwer-Lytton

Coconuts and palm trees,
Waves of calm emotion.
The wind is heard in the distance.
A whisper, a thought.

For he who brags never boasts,
And he who fears always falls.
The coming of ages,
The glory of disbelief,
The rise of spirit,
The dawn of Aquarius.

For you are not who you are,
But who you love.

Sit in stillness outdoors. Observe the sounds and waves of calmness. Allow nature to enter your being.

Day 355
We Are

"When men are inhuman, take care not to feel towards them as they do towards other humans."

Marcus Aurelius

Every day is different,
Even if it's the same.
Every moment is different,
Even if you've experienced it before.

Now is the only moment we have.
Now is the only moment we share.
Regret and guilt are our fears.
Happiness and togetherness are our goals.

We are the lucky.
We are the civil.
We are given names.
We are given things to do.
We have goals to attain.

We are human beings.

We are given one moment, and that is now. Stay present and humble, and never allow external circumstances to dictate your well-being.

Day 356
Be

"Beauty is in the eyes of the beholder."

Lie Zi

Beauty
Behold
Beyond
Become
Be.

You are beautiful, just like everything else in the world. Know this and appreciate all that is.

Day 357
Closeness

"Somewhere we know that without silence words lose their meaning, that without listening speaking no longer heals, that without distance closeness cannot cure."

Henri Nouwen

Every person you meet is an extension of yourself. The closer you are to someone, the closer you are to that portion of yourself. The closer you are with nature, the more open you are to infinite source. The more you know yourself, the closer you are to eternal happiness.

Feel the closeness of those around you. Be aware that everything and nothing is you.

Day 358
Random Events

"Every snowflake falls, each in its appropriate place."

Zen Proverb

There is no such thing as a random event.

Reflect on this. Know that within you is infinite intelligence.

Day 359
Loved Ones

"Let your love be like the misty rains, coming softly, but flooding the river."

Malagasy Proverb

Hold your loved ones close to your heart at all times. Be grateful and appreciative that you have people to love. Some live in isolation with no contact from others. You are fortunate to have someone to care for and someone who cares for you. No matter who you are, the most valuable and significant part of life will always be your loved ones. Unconditional love is the highest form of vibration we humans can attain. This does not come by effort. It comes from purity of heart. One must be sincere, generous, selfless, kind, and gentle. When one is of the essence of this kind of love, the family of loved ones grows to not only immediate family and friends, but to humanity. In order to attain this greatness, we must first love ourselves.

You are your loved ones, and those you do not care for. You are everything and nothing at the same time. Love and be loved.

Day 360
Times to Come

"Who among you will give ear to this? Who will hearken, and hear for the time to come?"

Isaiah 42:23

We are light in human form.
On our journey home to where we're from.
We are brave, forged, and strong.
Lest we forget our roots are raw.

Let me be, and you be still.
Let you live, and life be calm.
Let us be, in harmony bliss.
Wishful thinking, there is no risk.

So here we stand.
Divided yet one.
An illusion to be revealed,
In times to come.

This reality is an illusion. All that matters is within you. No external circumstances will ever bring eternal joy. One day, you will no longer be human.

Day 361
Words Are Weak

"Action speaks louder than words but not nearly as often."

Mark Twain

Words are weak; action is strong.
Words are bleak, misleading, and wrong.
Words can be said and never meant.
Words can be broken and always spent.

Speak loudly and never be heard.
Use force, and grow weak.
Soft and gentle are embraced.
Loving action is triumphant.

Be as you are. There is power.
Be who you are. There is love.
Be and let be. There is patience.
Simply be. There is enlightenment.

Words are weak.

Always allow your actions to speak for you. Always be sincere and mean what you say. This is your true path to freedom.

Day 362
Fortunate

"We never taste happiness in perfection; our most fortunate successes are mixed with sadness."

Pierre Corneille

Fortunate to be in this time of now.
Fortunate to be innocent and ignorant.
To marvel at the beauty;
To gaze in complete wonder.

This is the essence of life.

Our fleeting moments are only a glimpse,
In a realm of infinite possibilities.
The task can seem so daunting.
The path often undefined.

Yet there is always hope.
There is always a way.
There is higher power.

We are the fortunate.
We are this moment.
We are human beings.
A marvel of the universe.

Being appreciative of everything is the first step toward inner peace. This is the transformational process unfolding. Be fortunate for who you are now.

Day 363
From the Dalai Lama

"May I become at all times, both now and forever
A protector for those without protection
A guide for those who have lost their way
A ship for those with oceans to cross
A bridge for those with rivers to cross
A sanctuary for those in danger
A lamp for those without light
A place of refuge for those who lack shelter
And a servant to all in need."

Dalai Lama

Use your inner strength to help others. We are all one united entity. We are God. Together we are infinite.

Day 364
Beauty

"And he said unto them, He that hath ears to hear, let him hear."

Mark 4:9

Beauty is all around. One needs only to open his or her eyes. We are surrounded by miracles, life and death. The outer world is a reflection of our inner being. We have together created this beautiful world. We are God. We are everything we see and everything we cannot. For what is beauty if it is not looked upon with conscious admiration? We are given the opportunity to see the universe in all its glory. Our limited viewpoint is that of a child. Our ignorance and limitations are our gifts. To contemplate the unfathomable, to reach for new heights, to be one with all that is. This is the beauty of life as a human being.

You are and always will be all things. Being and nonbeing intertwined as one. A beauty so magnificent it cannot be described in mere words.

DAY 365
ENDINGS

"Every new beginning comes from some other beginning's end."

Seneca

We live in a world where everything must end. This is the end of our journey together. We have grown and touched each other's lives. The joy of writing to you has allowed me to view the world in new and interesting ways. Your reading this has given me the hope of a new world of peace, joy, and happiness. You are a part of me, as I am part of you. Though our journey together has ended, it will never be over. Every ending has a new beginning. Every death is a new birth. It is my hope that our time together has been a learning experience, and that you are now a more gracious, patient, caring, and compassionate individual. You are beautiful. You are inspiring, powerful, and integral to all that is. You are more than you will ever come to know. Enjoy your precious time here, for it will eventually come to an end. Like all things, we will transform and move on. This lifetime will be another memory, a drop of water in a vast ocean of consciousness.

Good-bye to you, my dear reader. Until we meet again. I love you. God bless.

Bibliographic Notes

The following are suggested readings and sources used as references for the creation of this book. Although this book has been created mainly through years of experience and growth, the following works have guided and shaped the message that has been presented.

*All bible quotes are from The Holy Bible King James Version. Oxford New York: Oxford University Press, 1611.

All other quotations found using the Google search engine.

Byrne, Rhonda. *The Secret.* New York: Beyond Words Publishing, 2006.

Canfield, Jack. *The Success Principles: How to Get from Where You Are to Where You Want to Be.* New York: Harper Collins Publishers, 2005.

Dwoskin, Hale. *The Sedona Method: Your Key to Lasting Happiness, Success, Peace, and Emotional Well-Being.* Arizona: Sedona Press 2003–2009.

Dyer, Wayne. *Getting in the Gap: Making Conscious Contact with God Through Meditation.* Carlsbad: Hay House, 1998.

Goldberg, Bruce. *Karmic Capitalism: A Spiritual Approach to Financial Independence.* Baltimore: Publish America, 2005.

Greene, Robert. *The 48 Laws of Power.* New York: Penguin, 1998.

Heaven, Ross. *The Spiritual Practices of the Ninja: Mastering the Four Gates to Freedom.* Vermont: Destiny Books, 2006.

Hill, Napoleon. *Think and Grow Rich.* New York: Ballantine, 1960.

Huang, Alfred, trans. *The Complete I Ching.* Rochester, Vermont: Inner Traditions, 2004.

Kehoe, John. *Mind Power into the Twenty-First Century: Techniques to Harness the Astounding Powers of Thought.* Vancouver: Zoetic Inc., 1997.

Levintin, Daniel J. *This Is Your Brain on Music: The Science of a Human Obsession.* New York: Penguin, 2006

Melchizedek, Drunvalo. *The Ancient Secret of the Flower of Life, Volume 1.* Flagstaff: Light Technology Publishing, 1990.

Melchizedek, Drunvalo. *The Ancient Secret of the Flower of Life, Volume 2.* Flagstaff: Light Technology Publishing, 2000.

Pealer, Grant H. *Worlds Beyond Death.* Huntsville: Ozark Mountain Publishing, 2007.

Pearce, Joseph. *The Crack in the Cosmic Egg: New Constructs of Mind and Reality.* Rochester: Park Street Press, 2002.

Proctor, Bob. *It's Not About the Money.* Toronto: Burman Books Inc., 2008.

Sams, Gregory. *Sun of gOd: Discover the Self-Organizing Consciousness That Underlies Everything.* San Francisco: Weiser Books, 2009.

Schaef, Anne Wilson. *Meditations for Living in Balance: Daily Solutions for People Who Do Too Much.* San Francisco: Harper Collins, 2000.

Tolle, Eckhart. *A New Earth: Awakening to Your Life's Purpose.* New York: Penguin, 2006.

Tolle, Eckhart. *The Power of Now: A Guide to Spiritual Enlightenment.* Vancouver: Namaste Publishing, 1997.

Tzu, Chang. *The Tao of Nature.* London: Penguin, 1996.

Tzu, Lao. *Tao Te Ching,* Hinton, David, trans. Washington: Counterpoint, 2000.

INDEX

*Titles **written in bold** are inspired by Alfred Huang's translation of the I Ching. For more information please refer to the bibliographic notes on page 385.

About the Author

Mark William Pezzelato was born on March 11, 1981, in Scarborough, Ontario. He is a musician, author, performer, and independent business owner. Mark has an honors degree graduating at the top of his class in announcing from the radio broadcasting program at Loyalist College in Belleville. He has studied human behavior as a self-exploration project and has taken psychology and philosophy courses at York University. In 2003 Mark founded Pezmosis Music Productions, a company focused on expanding and developing independent Canadian talent. Mark is often referred to as "Pez" amongst his friends. He plays drums for various rock, rap, and punk bands, and is the singer/songwriter of Vanek, an alternative rock band focused on the message of love and respect. He scores music for film and television and is well versed in many areas of expertise. Mark has a fascination for human behavior, healing, learning, growing, and evolving. Mark currently resides in Oak Ridges, Ontario.

You can contact Mark by
e-mailing pez@pezmosis.com.: